THE POWER OF THE MILLIONAIRE MINDSET

Edimilson Franca

CONTENTS

Title Page
The Power of the Millionaire Mindset ... 1
Chapter 1: The Beginning of the Journey - Dreaming Big ... 7
2: The Power of the Creative Mind ... 13
Chapter 3: The Importance of Habits for Success ... 19
Chapter 4: The Art of Resilience: Overcoming Adversity on the Path to Success ... 25
Chapter 5: Vision and Planning: Charting the Path to Success ... 31
Chapter 6: The Growth Mindset: Turning Challenges into Opportunities ... 37
Chapter 7: Innovation and Creativity: The Secret to Outperforming the Competition ... 43
Chapter 8: Networking Strategies: Building Valuable Relationships for Success ... 49
Chapter 9: The Art of Decision Making: How to Make Strategic and Effective Choices ... 55
Chapter 10: Innovation and Creativity: Cultivating the Mindset that Drives Success ... 61
Chapter 11: Networking and Building Relationships: The Power of Connections in Entrepreneurial Succe ... 67
Chapter 12: Time Management and Productivity: Maximizing the Enjoyment of Your Day ... 74

Chapter 13: Resilience and Overcoming: How to Face Adversity and Stay Focused — 80

Chapter 14: Resilience and Adaptation: Overcoming Adversity and Change — 86

Chapter 15: Legacy and Impact: Building a Lasting Future — 92

The Path to the Millionaire Mindset — 98

THE POWER OF THE MILLIONAIRE MINDSET

Introduction:

The millionaire mindset is much more than a simple desire to accumulate wealth. It is a way of thinking, acting and living that transcends material pursuits and touches the heart of personal development, professional fulfillment and lasting impact on the world. It is a mindset that differentiates those who achieve the extraordinary from those who remain ordinary. And what makes it so powerful is its ability to transform seemingly unattainable dreams into concrete realities.

In this book, we will explore the many facets of the millionaire mindset and how it can be developed, cultivated and used as a driver for success. The central idea is not just to get rich financially, but to enrich life as a whole, creating a lasting legacy and contributing positively to the world.

But what exactly is this *Millionaire Mentality*? How does it differ from common mindsets and why is it so crucial for anyone seeking not just success, but the true meaning of success? To understand this, we first need to demystify the notion that financial success is the only goal of those who think like millionaires. In reality, the millionaire mindset encompasses a vision of life that includes freedom, fulfillment, purpose, and the ability to positively impact other people.

The Foundation of the Millionaire Mindset: Thinking Big

Thinking big is the foundation of the millionaire mindset. Many of us grow up with limiting beliefs that condition us to accept what is "realistic" or "possible" within a narrow framework of possibilities. We are taught not to dream too big, not to reach beyond what is immediately in front of us. However, those who develop a millionaire mindset reject these self-imposed limits.

These individuals allow themselves to dream big, envisioning goals and objectives that others would consider impractical or out of reach. They are not afraid to set bold goals and pursue success on a scale most people would never dare imagine. This does not mean that they live in a fantasy disconnected from reality, but rather that they have an expanded vision of what is possible and are willing to work tirelessly to turn that vision into reality.

The Role of Habits in Forming a Millionaire Mindset

In addition to dreaming big, millionaire mindsets understand the crucial role of habits in shaping success. They know that success is not a one-off event, but the result of consistent, intentional practices over time. It is through habits that they shape their minds, bodies and environments to foster growth and fulfillment.

These habits are not only related to hard work or dedication to one's career, but also include self-development practices, such as constant reading, continuous learning and taking care of one's physical and mental well-being. The millionaire mindset involves creating a routine that supports high performance and, over time, builds the foundation for great achievements.

The Creative Mind: The Differentiator of

Successful Entrepreneurs

Another essential component of the millionaire mindset is the power of the creative mind. Creativity is not exclusive to artists or technology innovators; it is an indispensable tool for anyone who wants to achieve success in any area. Creativity allows entrepreneurs to see opportunities where others see problems, to find innovative solutions to seemingly insurmountable challenges, and to quickly adapt to change.

Successful entrepreneurs use their creative mind to innovate, take risks and differentiate themselves in the market. They are able to think outside the box and, most importantly, transform these creative ideas into practical strategies that generate results. The millionaire mindset, therefore, is not just about thinking big, but also about thinking differently, daring to challenge the status quo and break new ground.

Overcoming Limiting Beliefs: The First Big Challenge

One of the biggest barriers to developing a millionaire mindset is the presence of limiting beliefs. These are the inner voices that tell us we are not good enough, that success is for others, that the risk is too great, or that failure is inevitable. Limiting beliefs are like mental anchors that keep us grounded when we should be flying high.

Overcoming these beliefs is one of the first and most important steps on the journey to developing a millionaire mindset. This requires deep introspection and a willingness to confront and reprogram those negative thoughts. It's not an easy process, but it's absolutely necessary. Many of the world's most successful entrepreneurs talk openly about the battles they fought against their own doubts and fears before achieving success.

The Clear Vision: Targeting the Potential for Success

One of the most striking traits of those who have a millionaire mindset is the ability to develop and sustain a clear vision of where they want to go. This vision is not just a vague goal or a passing wish; it is an accurate and detailed representation of the future they want to create. It is this vision that guides their decisions, motivates their actions and keeps them firm even in the face of challenges.

Having a clear vision is like having a detailed map to success. Without it, it's easy to get lost in the countless obstacles and distractions that arise along the way. But with a well-defined vision, entrepreneurs are able to maintain focus and direction, knowing exactly what they are looking for and why they are willing to make the sacrifices necessary to get there.

Unshakable Confidence: Belief in One's Potential

Confidence is another fundamental pillar of the millionaire mindset. It is not just superficial or arrogant confidence, but a deep and unshakable belief in one's own potential. Those who achieve extraordinary success know that no matter what challenges they may face, they have the ability to find solutions and continue moving forward.

This trust is built over time, through experiences of overcoming and victories, big and small. Each achievement reinforces this internal belief, creating a virtuous cycle where confidence leads to success, which in turn, increases confidence even further. This self-confidence mindset is what allows entrepreneurs to face risks, overcome their fear of failure, and continue to pursue their goals with determination.

The Power of Connections: Networking and Collaboration

On the path to success, no one reaches the top alone. Connections and networking play a crucial role in any successful entrepreneur's journey. People with a millionaire mindset understand the importance of building and nurturing valuable relationships, whether they are with mentors, business partners, or even competitors.

These connections are not only sources of support, but also of new opportunities, ideas and perspectives. Having a powerful network allows entrepreneurs to expand their possibilities, learn from others' experiences, and find collaborative solutions to common challenges. The millionaire mentality values the strength of the collective, understanding that shared success is often more significant and lasting.

Resilience: The Ability to Get Up After Falls

Resilience is the ability to recover quickly from difficulties and is an indispensable characteristic for anyone who wants to achieve success on a large scale. In the world of business and entrepreneurship, failure is an inevitable reality. Those with a millionaire mindset, however, see failure not as an end, but as an opportunity to learn and grow.

These individuals are able to get back up after every fall, stronger and more determined than before. Resilience is what allows them to keep moving forward, even when things get difficult, and it is one of the traits that most distinguishes successful entrepreneurs from others.

Conclusion: An Invitation to Transformation

Throughout this book, we will explore each of these elements and many others that make up the millionaire mindset. You will discover how to develop these traits in yourself, applying them in your life and career to achieve extraordinary success. More than that, this book is an invitation to transform not just the way you think about success, but the way you live, act, and impact the world around you.

The journey to a millionaire mindset is not easy, but it is one of the most rewarding you can undertake. It requires courage, commitment and a willingness to challenge your own limits. But if you're willing to take that step, the rewards are immeasurable.

So let's start this journey together. Get ready to expand your horizons, break down mental barriers and unlock the limitless potential that lies within you. The millionaire mindset is within your reach, and this book will be your guide to achieving it and using it to create a life of success, fulfillment, and lasting impact.

CHAPTER 1: THE BEGINNING OF THE JOURNEY - DREAMING BIG

Extraordinary success never begins with timid steps; it always begins with a big dream, a burning desire that cannot be contained. At the heart of every successful entrepreneur lies the ability to dream beyond what the eyes can see, to envision a future that, for many, seems impossible or impractical. This chapter is dedicated to the transformative power of dreaming big, and how this ability to envision something bigger than the present is the first step in building a millionaire mindset.

Dreaming Big: The Seed of Success

Dreaming big is not just a matter of ambition or desire. It is a mental attitude that reflects a deep belief in the possibility of transforming what is imagined into reality. Those who dream big are not limited by current circumstances; rather, they see beyond immediate constraints, envisioning a future where their boldest aspirations become tangible.

For example, Steve Jobs, one of the greatest visionaries of our time, dreamed of putting a computer in every person's hands, at a time when most people didn't even know what a personal computer was. He did not limit himself to what was considered possible at the time, but persisted in his vision until it became a global reality. His ability to dream big is what drove him to challenge norms, radically innovate, and eventually transform the technology industry.

Likewise, Oprah Winfrey, who began her life under adverse circumstances, dreamed of becoming one of the most influential personalities in the world. She envisioned a future where she would not only overcome the barriers imposed by society, but also help millions of others overcome their own difficulties. Her journey is a testament to how dreaming big can inspire actions that change the course of one person's life and, by extension, many others.

Dreaming big is the seed of success because, without a clear and ambitious vision, it is impossible to achieve something truly remarkable. But what differentiates those who only dream from those who realize is the willingness to act on those dreams, transforming ideas into strategies and, eventually, into concrete results.

Challenging the Status Quo

A common trait among those with a millionaire mindset is a willingness to challenge the status quo. They are not content with what already exists or what is conventionally accepted; instead, they are constantly questioning, exploring and innovating. This desire to challenge established norms is what often leads to the creation of something new and revolutionary.

Take for example Elon Musk, an entrepreneur who has repeatedly challenged the industries he has involved himself in. Whether creating electric cars with Tesla, revolutionizing space exploration with SpaceX, or pursuing sustainable energy with

SolarCity, Musk stood out because he didn't accept the limitations of what was considered possible. He dreamed big and challenged the status quo, believing he could create solutions to problems that many considered insoluble.

Challenging the status quo requires courage and, often, a willingness to face criticism and skepticism. Those with a millionaire mindset are aware that the path to success often passes through unexplored territory and that the greatest rewards come to those who dare to tread new paths.

Visualization: Turning Dreams into Goals

Visualizing is more than just dreaming; is the process of transforming a desire or aspiration into a clear and specific goal. Visualization is a powerful tool used by many successful entrepreneurs to maintain focus and motivation on their journeys. When you visualize your goal clearly, you are creating a mind map that guides your actions and decisions, making the path to success more tangible and achievable.

A classic example of visualization in action is that of Arnold Schwarzenegger, who, before becoming a movie star and politician, was a champion bodybuilder. From a young age, Schwarzenegger envisioned his success, not only in bodybuilding, but also as a global icon. He used visualization as a technique to mentally prepare himself for each competition and challenge he faced. His ability to clearly see his goals has helped him overcome obstacles and achieve a level of success that many would consider impossible.

Visualizing success is, therefore, a critical step in any entrepreneur's journey. It's not enough to just want something; you need to see it clearly in your mind, define what it looks like, and then work tirelessly to bring it into reality.

The Importance of Long-Term Vision

Dreaming big also means thinking long term. Those who have a millionaire mindset understand that true success is not achieved overnight, but is the result of years of effort, learning and perseverance. They have a long-term vision that guides them, even when immediate results are difficult to see.

Jeff Bezos, the founder of Amazon, exemplifies this mindset. From the beginning, Bezos had a long-term vision for Amazon, envisioning it as "the everything store." He knew that to achieve this vision he would need to go through many years of heavy investment and low profits, but he remained committed to his vision. Today, Amazon is one of the largest and most influential companies in the world, a testament to the power of a long-term vision supported by a big dream.

This long-term vision also helps maintain resilience in difficult times. When you have a clear vision of where you want to go, it's easier to stay the course, even when challenges seem insurmountable. This long-term perspective is a defining characteristic of a millionaire mindset, allowing entrepreneurs to continue moving forward, even in the face of adversity.

The Big Dream as a Driver of Innovation

Dreaming big is also a powerful driver of innovation. When you allow your mind to explore limitless possibilities, you pave the way for creativity and innovation. Many of the greatest technological and business advances in history were the result of people who dreamed big and were not satisfied with what already existed.

An example of this is the story of the Wright brothers, who dreamed of flying at a time when this idea was considered crazy. They faced countless failures and skepticism, but continued to dream big and innovate until, in 1903, they achieved the first controlled, sustained flight of a heavier-than-air aircraft. His innovation not only realized his dream, but also paved the way for modern aviation, transforming the way the world connects.

This spirit of innovation is essential for any entrepreneur seeking success on a large scale. Dreaming big is not just about envisioning a better future; it's about creating that future through innovation, challenging what's possible and constantly looking for ways to improve and evolve.

The Courage to Dream Big

Dreaming big requires courage. In a world where skepticism and negativity often prevail, it takes courage to stand out and believe in something that doesn't yet exist. The millionaire mentality is, to a large extent, built on this courage – the willingness to believe in the impossible, to face challenges with determination and not to give up, even when others doubt it.

A powerful example of courage in entrepreneurship is Sara Blakely, founder of Spanx. Before creating his multimillion-dollar company, Blakely worked selling fax machines door to door. But she had a big dream – to create a line of underwear that would revolutionize the market. Despite having no experience in the fashion industry and facing countless rejections, Blakely persisted. Her courage to dream big, even in the face of countless adversities, led her to build one of the most successful companies of the last decade.

This courage is fueled by a deep conviction in one's vision. Those who dream big don't allow the fear of failure to paralyze them; instead, they use it as fuel to move forward. They understand that failure is part of the journey and that each obstacle overcome brings them even closer to their goal.

Dream Big and Act Big

Dreaming big is just the first step; the second is to act big. It's not enough to just have a vision; it is necessary to transform it into action. This means adopting an execution mindset, where each step is aimed at getting closer to the end goal.

Jack Ma, the founder of Alibaba, is a classic example of someone who dreamed big and acted big. When he started, Ma had an ambitious vision – to create a platform that would connect buyers and sellers around the world. He knew this vision would require massive action, and that's exactly what he did. Despite facing numerous challenges, including a lack of funding and market resistance, Ma persisted, transforming his vision into one of the largest e-commerce companies in the world.

Action is what differentiates dreamers from doers. Those who possess a millionaire mindset don't just dream of success; they work tirelessly to achieve it. They are persistent, resilient and committed to executing their visions, knowing that every action takes them one step closer to their goals.

The Journey Begins with a Dream

In this first chapter, we explore the power of dreaming big as the starting point for any successful journey. Dreaming big is more than a simple aspiration; it is a mindset that shapes actions, decisions and, eventually, results. Those who dare to dream big are positioning themselves to achieve something truly extraordinary.

As we progress through this book, we'll explore how this ability to dream big intertwines with other elements of the millionaire mindset, creating a clear path to success. But for now, remember: success begins in the mind. Allow yourself to dream big, visualize your future clearly and prepare to act with determination and courage. The world belongs to those who dare to dream and work to turn their dreams into reality.

2: THE POWER OF THE CREATIVE MIND

The human mind is one of the most powerful tools ever created. She has the ability to turn dreams into reality, to find solutions to the most complex problems and to create innovations that change the world. However, for many, this creative capacity remains underutilized. At the heart of a millionaire mindset is understanding and harnessing the power of the creative mind. This chapter is dedicated to exploring how this strength can be developed, cultivated, and utilized to achieve success.

Understanding the Creative Mind

The creative mind is not limited to artists, inventors or writers. We all have an inherent capacity for creativity, but we don't always recognize it or use it to its full potential. A creative mind is one that sees possibilities where others see limitations, that finds innovative solutions to seemingly insoluble problems, and that is constantly exploring new ideas and perspectives.

Creativity is the essence of human progress. Without it, we would be stuck in the same routines, repeating the same mistakes, without ever moving forward or evolving. The creative mind is the engine of innovation, change and growth. For the successful entrepreneur, this creativity is not just desirable; is essential. It is creativity that allows companies to differentiate themselves in competitive markets, find new ways to meet customer needs and adapt to an ever-changing world.

Cultivating the Creative Mind

Creativity, contrary to what many think, is not an innate quality that some have and others do not. It is a skill that can be developed and improved. To cultivate a creative mind, it is necessary to adopt habits and practices that encourage innovation and the exploration of new ideas.

One of the most effective ways to cultivate creativity is to embrace curiosity. Curiosity is the desire to learn, explore and understand the world around us. When you're curious, you're constantly seeking new information, new experiences, and new perspectives. This incessant search for knowledge is what fuels creativity. The more you know, the more you can connect seemingly disconnected ideas, generating innovative solutions and valuable insights.

Leonardo da Vinci, considered one of the greatest creative geniuses in history, was known for his insatiable curiosity. He explored a wide variety of fields, from art to engineering, and this multidisciplinary curiosity fueled his creativity. He did not limit himself to a single field of knowledge, but was constantly seeking to learn and understand more about the world around him. This curiosity allowed him to make discoveries and innovations that were far ahead of his time.

Another crucial aspect of cultivating creativity is creating space for experimentation. Creativity flourishes in environments where there is freedom to test new ideas, make mistakes, and learn from those experiences. In many successful companies, a culture of experimentation is encouraged, allowing employees to explore new approaches and ideas without the fear of failure.

For example, Google is known for its culture of innovation, where employees are encouraged to dedicate 20% of their work time to personal projects that can benefit the company. This freedom to experiment and explore new ideas has led to the development of iconic products like Gmail and Google Maps. The lesson here is clear: creativity cannot flourish in a restrictive environment. You need to create space for experimentation and be willing to learn from mistakes along the way.

The Power of Imagination

Imagination is the lifeblood of the creative mind. It is through imagination that we are able to visualize the future, to see beyond what is immediately apparent and to create something new and different. Imagination is what allows us to dream big and see possibilities where others see only obstacles.

Walt Disney, the creator of one of the world's largest entertainment empires, is a shining example of the power of imagination. From a young age, Disney imagined a world where fantasy and reality met, creating experiences that transcend the ordinary. His imagination knew no bounds, and he did not allow the financial or technological constraints of the time to impede his vision. He firmly believed that "if you can dream it, you can do it". And it was this belief that led him to create some of the most iconic films and theme parks in the world.

Imagination also plays a crucial role in problem solving. When faced with a challenge, those with a creative mindset are able to utilize their imagination to find innovative solutions. They are not limited to traditional approaches but are constantly exploring new ways of solving problems. This ability to think "outside the box" is what often leads to success in highly competitive fields.

Overcoming Creative Blocks

Even the most creative minds face blocks at some point. These blocks can be caused by a variety of factors, such as stress, lack of inspiration, or excessive pressure. However, there are ways to overcome these obstacles and reignite the creative flow.

One of the most effective strategies for overcoming creative blocks is to change your environment. Sometimes creativity can be stifled by familiar or routine environments. Changing the scene, whether moving to a new location or changing the layout of your workspace, can help stimulate new ideas. Exposure to new visual and sensory stimuli can trigger creative associations that were previously unnoticed.

Another useful technique is to take an uncensored "brainstorming" approach. During a creative block, it is common for ideas to be immediately discarded because they seem impractical or unconventional. However, during brainstorming, all ideas must be accepted, regardless of how unusual they may seem. Often, it's the idea that initially seems absurd that ends up leading to the most innovative solution. The goal is to generate as many ideas as possible, without judging or discarding any of them until the process is complete.

Additionally, it is important to recognize that creative blocks are part of the creative process. They should not be feared or avoided, but rather embraced as an opportunity to reevaluate and renew one's approach. Often, moments of creative stagnation precede the most significant advances. With patience and persistence, it is possible to overcome these obstacles and emerge with new ideas and perspectives.

Creativity as a Competitive Advantage

In the business world, creativity is one of the greatest competitive advantages that a company or individual can have. In a saturated market where products and services often seem indistinguishable, creativity is what allows a brand to stand out. It is the engine of innovation, enabling companies to create unique products, innovative marketing campaigns and memorable customer experiences.

A clear example of how creativity can be a competitive advantage is Apple. From the beginning, Apple has stood out for its creative approach to design and technology. Steve Jobs, the company's co-founder, was known for his obsession with aesthetics and functionality, seeking to create products that were not only useful, but also beautiful. This combination of innovative design and cutting-edge technology has allowed Apple to stand out in a highly competitive market, creating a loyal and passionate customer base.

Creativity can also be a competitive advantage in the way companies approach challenges. Instead of following the same strategies as everyone else, creative companies are willing to think differently and adopt unconventional approaches. This can manifest itself in everything from the way a company manages its staff to the way it interacts with its customers.

For example, Zappos, a shoe e-commerce company, is known for its creative approach to customer service. Instead of following industry standard practices, Zappos has created a culture where customer service is the top priority. They offer generous return policies, intensive training for their employees, and a willingness to go the extra mile to satisfy customers. This creative approach to customer service has helped Zappos build a stellar reputation and differentiate itself in a competitive market.

Creativity and Resilience

Creativity is also closely linked to resilience. In a business environment that is constantly changing, the ability to adapt and innovate is crucial. Those with a creative mindset are able to see opportunities where others see challenges. They are flexible and willing to change their approaches as necessary to adapt to new circumstances.

The Netflix story is a perfect example of how creativity can be used to overcome challenges and adapt to a changing market. Originally a DVD rental company, Netflix realized that the future of entertainment was in digital streaming. Rather than resist change, the company embraced innovation, transforming itself from a DVD rental company into one of the largest streaming services in the world. This ability to innovate and adapt to new market realities is what has allowed Netflix to not only survive, but thrive in a highly competitive environment.

Creative resilience is what allows entrepreneurs not to give up when faced with obstacles. They understand that failure is part of the process and that each setback is an opportunity to learn, grow and find new solutions. A creative mindset, combined with resilience, is what allows entrepreneurs to overcome challenges and continue moving towards success.

Unleashing the Power of the Creative Mind

The power of the creative mind is limitless. When cultivated and used correctly, creativity can turn dreams into reality, solve the most difficult problems and create innovations that change the world. For successful entrepreneurs, creativity is not just a desirable skill; it is a necessity. It is through creativity that ideas become actions, that challenges become opportunities and that dreams become achievements.

By the end of this chapter, I hope you are inspired to explore and cultivate your own creative mind. Remember that creativity is a skill that can be developed and improved with practice and dedication. The more you exercise your creative mind, the more powerful it becomes. And with this strength in your hands, there is no limit to what you can achieve. The world is full of possibilities, and it's up to you to unleash the power of your creative mind to turn those possibilities into reality.

CHAPTER 3: THE IMPORTANCE OF HABITS FOR SUCCESS

While creativity and imagination are powerful forces that drive success, they need to be anchored in consistent habits to produce tangible results. In the world of business and entrepreneurship, habits are not just daily routines; they are the foundations on which careers, businesses, and fortunes are built. In this chapter, we'll explore the importance of habits in developing a millionaire mindset and how these habits can be formed, maintained, and improved over time.

The Role of Habits in Success

Habits are behaviors that we repeat regularly and often unconsciously. They are powerful because, once established, they require little mental energy to maintain. This means that the right habits can allow you to steadily move towards your goals without the conscious effort that would be required if each action was deliberate.

In the context of the millionaire mindset, habits play a crucial role. They are the building blocks of sustainable success. While talent and luck may play temporary roles, it is the consistency of daily habits that sustains long-term success. As author and entrepreneur Jim Rohn said, "Success is nothing more than a few simple disciplines, practiced every day." This discipline, rooted in good habits, is what differentiates those who achieve great things from those who fall short of their potential.

Forming Powerful Habits

Habit formation does not happen by chance; it is an intentional process that requires discipline, self-awareness, and patience. To form powerful habits, you must first identify which specific actions will contribute to your long-term success.

An example of a key habit for many successful entrepreneurs is regular reading. Warren Buffett, one of the most successful investors in the world, attributes much of his success to his reading habit. He spends around 80% of his day reading and believes this habit is essential for staying informed and making better decisions. Buffett once said, "Read 500 pages every day. That's how knowledge works. It accumulates, like compound interest." This is a clear example of how a simple habit, maintained over time, can have a profound impact on a person's success trajectory.

Another example is the practice of setting daily goals. Tony Robbins, one of the greatest life and business coaches in the world, defends the importance of starting the day with a clear vision of what you want to achieve. He suggests that by setting specific goals for the day, you are training your mind to focus on what's important and to take consistent action toward those goals. Robbins teaches that "repetition is the mother of skill," suggesting that by repeating certain actions daily, you are conditioning yourself for success.

To form a new habit, experts suggest starting small and gradually increasing the frequency or intensity of the action. For example, if you want to adopt a daily exercise habit, start with a modest goal, such as 10 minutes of walking per day. As this habit takes root, you can gradually increase the time or intensity of your exercise. The important thing is to maintain consistency, as it is through regular repetition that habits become solid.

Maintaining and Refining Habits

Maintaining a habit is as important as forming it. One of the most common challenges people face is the difficulty of maintaining new habits over the long term. Often, a new habit is followed diligently for a few weeks, but then abandoned when challenges or distractions arise.

The key to maintaining habits long-term is creating support systems that help reinforce these behaviors. One of these systems is the use of "triggers" – signals that indicate it is time to do the habit. For example, if your goal is to meditate daily, you can use the habit of brushing your teeth in the morning as a trigger to start your meditation session. Over time, the act of brushing your teeth will automatically signal to your brain that it's time to meditate, making it easier to maintain the habit.

Another effective system is record keeping or diaries. Recording your progress daily can provide a sense of accomplishment and responsibility, which helps you maintain momentum. Seeing your progress accumulate over time makes you more motivated to continue, even on days when your initial motivation wanes.

Furthermore, it is important to be aware that habits must be flexible and adaptable. As your circumstances and goals change, you may need to adjust your habits to ensure they continue to support your success. For example, the habit of reading for an hour every morning may need to be adjusted if your daily responsibilities change. Instead of giving up the habit completely, you might decide to split your reading into two 30-minute sessions at different times of the day.

Examples of Success Habits

Let's now explore some specific habits that are often mentioned by successful entrepreneurs and leaders as being fundamental to their millionaire mindset.

1. Get up early: Many successful leaders, such as Apple CEO Tim Cook and Virgin Group founder Richard Branson, are known for waking up early. This habit gives them a calm and productive start to the day, allowing them to accomplish important tasks before the demands of everyday life begin to arise. The practice of waking up early is also associated with better mental focus and a feeling of control over the day.

2. Regular physical exercise: Physical exercise is not only important for physical health, but also for mental health. Leaders like Barack Obama and Oprah Winfrey incorporate exercise into their daily routines because they know that exercise helps reduce stress, increase energy, and improve mental clarity. This habit ensures that they maintain high levels of energy and resilience, essential for facing daily challenges.

3. Meditation or mindfulness: The practice of meditation or mindfulness has become increasingly popular among business leaders as a way to manage stress and improve focus. Ray Dalio, founder of Bridgewater Associates, and Jeff Weiner, CEO of LinkedIn, are advocates of meditation as a habit that improves decision-making and promotes calm in high-pressure environments. This habit helps develop a more focused and resilient mind, capable of dealing with challenges more effectively.

4. Daily planning and reflection: Taking time to plan the day and reflect on achievements and learnings is a common habit among successful people. Robin Sharma, author of "The Monk Who Sold His Ferrari," suggests that daily planning is essential to ensure you're always moving toward your goals. Daily reflection also allows you to identify areas for improvement and adjust your strategies as needed.

5. Intentional Networking: Cultivating strong, meaningful relationships is another habit that many successful leaders prioritize. They understand that success is not just what you know, but also who you know. Leaders like Elon Musk and Bill Gates take the time to build and maintain a network of influential contacts by attending events, mentoring others, and collaborating on projects.

Breaking Negative Habits

While forming positive habits is crucial to success, it is equally important to identify and eliminate negative habits that may be sabotaging your progress. Negative habits like procrastination, lack of organization, or constant distractions can undermine your efforts and prevent you from reaching your full potential.

The first step to breaking a negative habit is recognizing it and understanding the impact it has on your life. Often, we are so used to our behaviors that we don't even realize the damage they cause. An effective way to identify these habits is to keep an activity diary for a week, noting how you spend your time and which repetitive behaviors are present.

Once you've identified a negative habit, the next step is to replace it with a positive habit. For example, if you have a habit of constantly checking social media while working, you can replace this behavior with time slots dedicated to deep focus, where you turn off all distractions and focus completely on the task at hand.

Changing negative habits requires patience and persistence. It is important not to judge yourself harshly when relapses occur. Instead, view each misstep as a learning opportunity and adjust your strategies as needed. Over time, as you replace negative habits with positive ones, you will create a stronger foundation for success.

The Success Foundation

Habits are the foundations upon which success is built. They are the small daily actions that, accumulated over time, lead to big achievements. For those looking to develop a millionaire mindset, it's essential to focus on forming, maintaining, and refining habits that support your long-term goals.

By the end of this chapter, I hope you have a clearer understanding of the importance of habits in developing your mindset and career. Remember that success is not the result of large, sporadic actions, but rather the accumulation of small, consistent actions over time. With the right habits, you can build a life of success, prosperity and fulfillment.

CHAPTER 4: THE ART OF RESILIENCE: OVERCOMING ADVERSITY ON THE PATH TO SUCCESS

Resilience is one of the most crucial characteristics for any entrepreneur seeking to achieve success. On the path to becoming a millionaire, you will inevitably face challenges, obstacles and failures. How you deal with these adversities will determine your long-term success. This chapter is dedicated to the art of resilience – how to develop it, cultivate it, and apply it on your journey to the millionaire mindset.

What is Resilience?

Resilience is the ability to recover quickly from difficulties. It's not just about surviving challenges, but also thriving despite them. In the business world, resilience means being able to continue to pursue your goals, even when everything seems to be going against you. It's the ability to pick yourself up after a failure, learn from the experience and move forward with more strength and determination.

Resilience is not an innate quality; it can be developed and strengthened over time. Contrary to what many think, being resilient does not mean being insensitive or indifferent to pain or failure. Instead, it's the ability to face those difficult experiences, process them in a healthy way, and use what you've learned to move forward.

Resilience in Action: Examples of Great Leaders

History is full of examples of leaders who faced extreme adversity but managed to overcome them thanks to their resilience. A notable example is that of Steve Jobs. Expelled from the company he founded, Jobs could have given up and followed a different path. However, he used this painful experience as an opportunity to learn and grow. Jobs founded NeXT and acquired Pixar, both companies that played key roles in his triumphant return to Apple. His resilience not only helped him overcome rejection, but also propelled him to lead one of the greatest business turnarounds in history.

Another example is that of Elon Musk. Known for his ambition and vision of the future, Musk faced numerous difficulties on his journey. From the near bankruptcy of Tesla and SpaceX to public derision and the failure of multiple projects, Musk could have given up countless times. However, his resilience allowed him to persevere, turning challenges into opportunities and eventually leading the technological revolution in several industries.

These examples show that resilience is a key factor in long-term success. Regardless of the obstacles you face, it is your ability to get up and keep going that will determine your destiny.

Building Resilience: Practical Strategies

Developing resilience is an ongoing process that requires effort and practice. Here are some practical strategies to strengthen your resilience and prepare you to face adversity on the path to success.

1. Change your mindset about failure: The first step to developing resilience is changing your perspective on failure. Instead of seeing failure as something to be avoided at all costs, see it as a learning opportunity. Every time you fail, you learn something new about yourself, your business and the world around you. Adopting a growth mindset – the belief that you can improve and grow over time – is essential to cultivating resilience.

2. Develop self-awareness: Self-awareness is the ability to recognize and understand your own feelings, thoughts and behaviors. Developing self-awareness allows you to identify how you respond to stress and adversity, which is crucial to strengthening your resilience. Practices like meditation, daily reflection, and therapy can help improve your self-awareness. The more you know yourself, the more prepared you will be to face challenges calmly and clearly.

3. Build a support network: Having a strong support network is essential for resilience. This can include friends, family, mentors and co-workers who are there to offer emotional support and practical advice when you face difficulties. A support network not only provides comfort during difficult times, but also offers different perspectives and insights that can help you overcome challenges. Additionally, sharing your experiences with others can help relieve stress and strengthen your resolve.

4. Practice adapting: Resilience involves the ability to adapt to new circumstances and changes. In an ever-changing world, being able to adjust your plans and strategies is essential to success. This means being willing to step out of your comfort zone, try new approaches, and learn from your mistakes. The more you practice adapting, the more natural it will become, strengthening your resilience over time.

5. Cultivate patience and persistence: Resilience not only means recovering quickly, but also having the patience to face long-term challenges. Success often doesn't come immediately, and it takes persistence to keep working toward your goals, even when the results aren't immediate. Cultivating patience and persistence is essential to developing the resilience necessary to achieve long-term success.

6. Take care of your physical and mental health: Resilience is strengthened when you are physically and mentally healthy. Taking care of your physical health – through regular exercise, a balanced diet and adequate sleep – has a direct impact on your ability to deal with stress and recover from adversity. Likewise, taking care of your mental health – through practices such as meditation, reading and relaxation – is crucial to maintaining mental clarity and emotional strength.

Overcoming Adversity: Case Studies

To illustrate the power of resilience, let's examine two case studies of entrepreneurs who faced significant adversity but managed to overcome it and achieve success.

1. Howard Schultz and the Creation of Starbucks: Howard Schultz, the visionary behind Starbucks, faced numerous challenges before transforming the small coffee shop into a global brand. Schultz grew up in a poor neighborhood and faced financial difficulties from an early age. When he decided to invest in Starbucks, he faced resistance from both investors and his own colleagues. Yet Schultz persisted, convinced he could create a new coffee culture in the United States. Even after several failed attempts and moments of crisis, he continued to believe in his vision. His resilience allowed him to overcome difficulties and transform Starbucks into a global empire.

2. J.K. Rowling and the Success of Harry Potter: J.K. Rowling, author of the famous Harry Potter series, is another example of resilience in action. Before achieving success, Rowling faced years of financial difficulties, editorial rejections and personal crises.

She wrote the first book in the series while struggling as a single mother and living on welfare. Despite numerous rejections from publishers, Rowling did not give up on her dream of publishing the book. Her resilience was rewarded when she finally found a publisher willing to take a chance on her work, and Harry Potter became a global phenomenon, transforming Rowling's life and inspiring millions of readers around the world.

These case studies show that resilience not only helps overcome adversity, but can also lead to unexpected opportunities and extraordinary success.

Resilience in the Modern Era

In the modern world, resilience is more important than ever. We live in an era of rapid change, where uncertainty and volatility are the norm. From global economic crises to disruptive technological advances, the challenges we face today require unprecedented resilience.

Entrepreneurs who want to thrive in this era must be prepared to face a variety of adversities. This includes not only financial and operational challenges, but also issues related to mental health, sustainability and ethics. Those who can adapt, learn from their experiences, and maintain a resilient mindset are best positioned to achieve long-term success.

Resilience in the modern era also involves the ability to reinvent oneself. With the rapid evolution of industries and technologies, it is essential that entrepreneurs are willing to adapt and explore new opportunities. This could mean changing careers, pivoting a business, or learning new skills to stay relevant. The ability to reinvent yourself, combined with resilience, is a powerful combination that can lead to lasting success.

Strengthening your Resilience

Resilience is one of the most important skills you can develop on your journey to achieving a millionaire mindset. It allows you to face adversity with courage, learn from your failures, and continue moving towards your goals.

By the end of this chapter, I hope you are more aware of the importance of resilience in your life and career. Developing resilience is not a quick or easy process, but it is essential to achieving long-term success. With practice and time, you can strengthen your resilience and prepare to face any challenge life throws your way.

CHAPTER 5: VISION AND PLANNING: CHARTING THE PATH TO SUCCESS

A millionaire mindset isn't just about having great ideas; It's also about having a clear vision and a detailed plan to turn those ideas into reality. Vision and planning are the pillars that support the achievement of ambitious goals and the construction of a solid path to success. In this chapter, we will explore the importance of having a well-defined vision and practicing effective strategic planning. We'll discuss how to develop a powerful vision and create a plan that guides you on your journey to success.

The Importance of Vision

Vision is the ability to imagine a desired future and clearly articulate what you want to achieve. It is the driving force behind great undertakings and achievements. Without a clear vision, you can get lost along the way, straying from your goals and succumbing to distractions and uncertainty.

A powerful vision not only provides clear direction but also serves as a source of inspiration and motivation. When you have a clear vision of where you want to go, every action and decision becomes a step towards that destination. Vision acts as a guide, helping you maintain focus and determination even when challenges arise.

Inspiring Example: Successful Visionaries

A notable example of a successful vision is that of Jeff Bezos, founder of Amazon. From the start, Bezos had an ambitious vision to transform Amazon from an online bookstore into a global e-commerce giant. Their vision included not only expanding the range of products offered, but also creating an exceptional shopping experience for customers. Bezos said, "If you do a good job, customers will tell their friends. If you do a great job, they will tell everyone." This long-term vision and commitment to excellence has helped transform Amazon into one of the most valuable companies in the world.

Another example is Elon Musk and his vision for SpaceX. Musk imagined a new era of space exploration and the possibility of colonizing Mars. His vision not only propelled him to overcome significant technical and financial challenges, but also inspired a new generation of entrepreneurs and scientists. Musk's vision of making interplanetary life a reality continues to guide his efforts and innovations.

Developing a Clear Vision

Developing a clear and inspiring vision is a process that requires reflection, introspection and strategic planning. Here are some steps to help you create a powerful vision for your life and career:

1. Reflect on your values and passions: To create a vision that resonates with you, it's essential to start by reflecting on what's truly important to you. What are your core values? What are you passionate about? Your vision should be aligned with your values and passions as this will ensure you are motivated and committed to your journey.

2. Identify your long-term goals: Think about where you want to be in 5, 10 or 20 years. What are your most ambitious goals? Your vision should reflect these goals and offer a clear picture of how you intend to achieve them. Having a long-term vision will help you stay focused and direct your daily actions towards achieving these goals.

3. Imagine your ideal future: Close your eyes and imagine the ideal future you want to create for yourself. What would your life be like if you achieved all your goals? What would be the characteristics of this ideal future? Use this vision to create a clear, detailed picture of what you want to achieve. The more vivid and specific your vision, the more powerful it becomes.

4. Write a vision statement: Once you have a clear vision in mind, write a vision statement that summarizes your goals and aspirations. This statement should be inspiring, motivating and easy to remember. A good vision statement acts as a constant reminder of your purpose and goals.

The Role of Strategic Planning

While the vision provides the direction, strategic planning provides the detailed roadmap to get there. Strategic planning is the process of setting goals, identifying necessary resources, and developing an action plan to achieve those goals. Effective planning is critical to turning your vision into reality and ensuring you are on the right path to success.

1. Set SMART Goals: SMART goals are an effective tool for strategic planning. SMART is an acronym that stands for:

- **S**specific   (Specific): The goal must be clear and specific.
- **M**ensurable   (Measurable): The goal must be quantifiable, allowing you to   track progress.

- **A**dyeable   (Attainable): The goal must be realistic and achievable.
- **R**elephants   (Relevant): The goal must be relevant to your long-term goals   term.
- **T**timeable (Temporal): The goal must have a   defined deadline.

For example, instead of setting a generic goal like "I want to grow my business," a SMART goal would be "increase sales by 20% in the next 12 months." This approach makes your goals more tangible and actionable, making planning and execution easier.

2. Create an Action Plan: A detailed action plan is essential to implementing your strategy. The plan should include specific steps you need to take to reach your goals, resources needed, and deadlines for each step. Break your goals into smaller, manageable tasks to make the process more organized and less intimidating.

3. Identify and Manage Resources: Strategic planning involves identifying and managing the resources needed to achieve your goals. This may include financial, human, technological and material resources. Make sure you have a clear understanding of the resources available and how to allocate them effectively.

4. Monitor and Evaluate Progress: Tracking progress is a crucial part of strategic planning. Establish metrics to evaluate your progress against established goals and regularly review your plan to ensure you're on track. If necessary, adjust your strategy to deal with unforeseen changes or challenges.

Overcoming Planning Challenges

While strategic planning is a powerful tool, it's important to be prepared to face challenges and obstacles along the way. Here are some strategies for dealing with planning challenges:

1. Adapt to Changes: The business environment is dynamic and can change quickly. Be prepared to adapt your plan as new opportunities or challenges arise. Flexibility is essential to ensure you can adjust your strategy as needed to continue moving towards your goals.

2. Manage Risks Proactively: Identify potential risks that could impact your plan and develop strategies to manage them. This may include creating contingency plans and implementing preventative measures to mitigate potential problems. Proactive risk management will help minimize the impact of unforeseen challenges.

3. Maintain Motivation and Focus: Maintaining motivation and focus is essential to overcoming challenges. Remember your vision and the reasons you are pursuing your goals. Use motivation techniques, such as visualizing success and celebrating small achievements, to maintain enthusiasm and determination along the way.

4. Seek Feedback and Learn from Experience: Seek feedback from mentors, peers, and experts to gain different perspectives and improve your plan. Learn from your experiences and be open to adjusting your approach based on what you learn along the journey. Continuous learning is essential for growth and adaptation.

The Path to Success

Vision and planning are essential to achieving a millionaire mindset and turning your dreams into reality. While vision provides direction and inspiration, strategic planning provides the roadmap and steps needed to achieve your goals. Developing a clear vision and creating a detailed plan are key steps to building a solid foundation for success.

By the end of this chapter, I hope you have a clearer understanding of the importance of vision and planning on your journey to success. Remember that having an inspiring vision and a well-crafted plan are powerful tools that will help you overcome challenges, stay focused, and achieve your most ambitious goals. With a clear vision and effective strategic planning, you will be prepared to face any challenge and move forward towards a life of success and fulfillment.

CHAPTER 6: THE GROWTH MINDSET: TURNING CHALLENGES INTO OPPORTUNITIES

A growth mindset is one of the most powerful qualities you can cultivate as you strive for success. This mindset, which contrasts with a fixed mindset, emphasizes the importance of seeing challenges as opportunities for growth and learning. In the context of business ventures and personal success, adopting a growth mindset can be the key to turning obstacles into stepping stones to success.

In this chapter, we will explore the concept of a growth mindset, how to develop it, and apply it to effectively face challenges. We'll also discuss how this mindset can influence your approach to continuous learning, innovation, and personal development.

What is the Growth Mindset?

Growth mindset, a concept popularized by psychologist Carol Dweck, is the belief that skills and intelligence can be developed through effort, practice, and learning. In contrast, a fixed mindset is the belief that our capabilities are innate and unchanging. Those with a fixed mindset tend to avoid challenges, give up easily, and feel threatened by the success of others.

The growth mindset, on the other hand, embraces challenges and sees failure as a learning opportunity. It is the belief that by dedicating yourself and working hard, you can improve and achieve your goals. This mindset is essential for facing the inevitable challenges that arise along the journey to success.

The Importance of Growth Mindset

Adopting a growth mindset can transform the way you face challenges and adversity. Here are some reasons why this mindset is critical to success:

1. Face Challenges with Courage: A growth mindset encourages you to face challenges with courage and determination. Instead of avoiding difficult situations, you see these experiences as opportunities to learn and improve. This allows you to take more risks and put yourself in situations that can lead to growth and innovation.

2. Learning from Failure: Failure is an inevitable part of any successful journey. With a growth mindset, you see failure as an opportunity to learn and grow rather than a reflection of your abilities or worth. This allows you to recover more quickly from setbacks and continue moving towards your goals.

3. Develop Skills and Competencies: The growth mindset emphasizes continuous learning and skill development. Instead of being content with the status quo, you constantly seek to improve your skills and acquire new knowledge. This not only increases your ability to face challenges, but also contributes to your long-term success.

4. Inspire and Motivate Others: By adopting a growth mindset, you become an example for others. Your willingness to face challenges and learn from experiences inspires and motivates those around you. This can create a more positive and productive work environment where everyone is committed to growth and continuous improvement.

Developing a Growth Mindset

Developing a growth mindset is a process that requires practice and dedication. Here are some strategies for cultivating this mindset in your life and career:

1. Embrace the Unknown: A growth mindset involves a willingness to face the unknown and explore new opportunities. Instead of avoiding situations that you don't master, seek to learn from these experiences. This could mean taking on new challenges at work, trying new approaches or acquiring new skills.

2. Reinterpret Failure: Change your perspective on failure. Instead of seeing it as a sign of incompetence, see it as a learning opportunity. Analyze what went wrong, identify key lessons, and use those lessons to improve your approach in the future. The ability to learn from failure is a fundamental characteristic of the growth mindset.

3. Cultivate Self-Knowledge: Self-knowledge is essential for developing a growth mindset. Be aware of your strengths and weaknesses, and recognize areas where you can improve. Use this awareness to set personal and professional growth goals and continually work towards achieving them.

4. Seek Feedback and Use It Constructively: Seek feedback from peers, mentors, and supervisors to get different perspectives on your performance. Instead of seeing feedback as criticism, use it as an opportunity to learn and improve. The ability to accept and use feedback constructively is an important part of the growth mindset.

5. Invest in Continuous Learning: Continuous learning is a fundamental aspect of the growth mindset. Constantly look for opportunities to acquire new knowledge and skills. This could include courses, workshops, reading books or attending conferences. By investing in your learning, you will be better prepared to face new challenges and opportunities.

Applying the Growth Mindset in Practice

Applying a growth mindset in your everyday life can have a significant impact on your approach to challenges and opportunities. Here are some ways to incorporate this mindset into your practice:

1. See Problems as Challenges: When faced with a problem, take a proactive approach and see it as a challenge to be overcome. Instead of feeling discouraged or overwhelmed, focus on finding solutions and learning from the experience. This approach not only helps you solve problems, but also strengthens your ability to face future challenges.

2. Set Learning Goals: Set specific goals related to learning and personal development. These goals should be challenging but achievable, and they should align with your long-term goals. By setting learning goals, you will be more motivated to seek new opportunities and expand your skills.

3. Develop Resilience Through Practice: Resilience is a skill that can be improved with practice. Engage in activities that challenge you and require persistence and effort. This could include long-term projects, challenging tasks at work, or activities you'd like to master. Constant practice will help strengthen your resilience and growth mindset.

4. Celebrate Your Achievements and Learnings: Recognize and celebrate your achievements and learnings along the way. This can include small victories, like completing a difficult project or developing a new skill. Celebrating these achievements helps you stay motivated and recognize the progress you've made.

Overcoming Barriers to the Growth Mindset

While the growth mindset offers many benefits, there can be barriers that make it difficult to adopt. Here are some strategies for overcoming these barriers:

1. Identify and Confront Limiting Beliefs: Limiting beliefs are thoughts and attitudes that prevent growth and change. Identify any negative beliefs that may be affecting your mindset and work to replace them with a more positive, constructive outlook. This may require introspection and the help of a mentor or coach.

2. Cultivate a Supportive Environment: Surround yourself with people who support and encourage your growth. A positive and supportive environment can reinforce your commitment to a growth mindset and provide motivation during challenging times.

3. Practice Self-Compassion: Self-compassion is the ability to be kind and understanding to yourself during difficult times. Instead of harshly criticizing yourself for mistakes or failures, treat yourself with the same kindness and understanding you would offer a friend. Self-compassion helps maintain a positive mindset and resilience.

4. Develop Perseverance: Perseverance is the ability to continue moving forward, even in the face of difficulties. Developing perseverance involves staying focused on your goals, even when things get difficult. The practice of overcoming obstacles and continuing to move forward will strengthen your growth mindset.

The Power of the Growth Mindset

A growth mindset is a powerful tool that can transform the way you face challenges and pursue success. By adopting a growth mindset, you become better able to see opportunities rather than obstacles, learn from failure, and continue to develop along your journey.

By the end of this chapter, I hope you have a deeper understanding of the concept of growth mindset and how to apply it in your life and career. Remember that a growth mindset is not a final destination, but an ongoing process of learning and adapting. Cultivating this mindset will help you face challenges with courage, seize opportunities for growth, and achieve your most ambitious goals.

With a growth mindset, you will be better prepared to turn challenges into opportunities and achieve the success you desire. Adopt this mindset and see how it can transform your life and career, guiding you to a future of achievement and success.

CHAPTER 7: INNOVATION AND CREATIVITY: THE SECRET TO OUTPERFORMING THE COMPETITION

Innovation and creativity are driving forces that drive success and differentiation in the competitive world of business and entrepreneurship. In an ever-changing environment, where new technologies and trends emerge all the time, the ability to innovate and think creatively is crucial to maintaining a competitive advantage and achieving extraordinary results. In this chapter, we will explore how innovation and creativity can be cultivated, applied, and used to outperform the competition and achieve success.

The Role of Innovation in Business Success

Innovation is the ability to create something new or significantly improve what already exists. In the business context, innovation can manifest itself in various forms, including new products, services, processes or business models. Companies that innovate are often able to stand out from the competition and create significant value for their customers.

1. The Importance of Innovation: Innovation is essential for the survival and long-term growth of any business. In a saturated market where many products and services are similar, innovation offers a way to differentiate yourself and create a unique value proposition. This not only attracts customers, but can also result in new revenue and growth opportunities.

Inspiring Example: Apple Inc.

Apple is an iconic example of how innovation can transform a company and the market. From the launch of the iPod to the iPhone and iPad, Apple has continually introduced revolutionary products that have redefined their respective categories. Innovation is not limited to products; Apple also innovated its business model with the App Store and iCloud, creating an integrated ecosystem that delivers value to customers and increases brand loyalty.

Cultivating Creativity

Creativity is the ability to generate new ideas and original solutions. While innovation involves the practical application of these ideas to create something new, creativity is the starting point of this process. Cultivating creativity is essential to generate innovative ideas and face challenges in an original way.

1. Creating an Environment Favorable for Creativity: An environment that stimulates creativity is essential for generating innovative ideas. This can include creating an inspiring physical space, promoting a culture of collaboration, and the freedom to experiment and explore new ideas. Allowing team members to share their ideas without fear of criticism is crucial to fostering a steady flow of creativity.

2. Encouraging Curiosity: Curiosity is a driving force behind creativity. Encourage curiosity by exploring new areas of knowledge, asking questions and challenging the status quo. Curiosity leads to new perspectives and can result in innovative solutions to existing problems.

3. Adopting Creative Thinking Techniques: There are several techniques to stimulate creative thinking, including brainstorming, mind maps and the "5 Whys" technique. These techniques help you explore different angles and generate a variety of ideas. Experimenting with different methods can help you find new ways to approach challenges and create innovative solutions.

4. Learning from Other Industries: Looking beyond your own industry can provide new ideas and inspiration. Many innovations arise from the application of concepts from one area to another. Studying how other companies and industries face challenges can offer valuable insights and new approaches to your own situation.

Applying Innovation to Your Business

Once you have cultivated creativity, it is essential to strategically apply innovation to your business. This involves identifying areas where innovation can add value, developing and implementing new solutions, and measuring results.

1. Identifying Innovation Opportunities: Assess your business to identify areas that could benefit from innovation. This may include internal processes, products or services offered, or the customer experience. Analyzing customer feedback and observing market trends can also reveal opportunities for innovation.

2. Developing an Innovation Plan: Create an innovation plan that describes how you intend to apply new ideas and solutions. The plan should include clear objectives, required resources, and a timeline for implementation. It is important to have a structured approach to ensure that innovation is integrated effectively into your business.

3. Testing and Refining Innovations: Before launching a new idea or product on a large scale, it is important to test it on a smaller scale. This allows you to identify and fix potential issues before a full release. Use feedback from testing to refine and improve the innovation before fully implementing it.

4. Measuring the Impact of Innovation: Measure the success of your innovations by measuring key performance indicators (KPIs) such as revenue growth, customer satisfaction and operational efficiency. This assessment will help you understand the impact of the innovation and adjust your strategies as necessary.

Overcoming Barriers to Innovation

Although innovation is essential, there are barriers that can hinder its implementation. Here are some strategies for overcoming these barriers and fostering a culture of innovation:

1. Overcome the Fear of Failure: Fear of failure can inhibit creativity and the willingness to innovate. Foster a culture where failure is seen as a learning opportunity rather than a negative consequence. Encourage experimentation and continuous learning, and recognize that failure is a normal part of the innovation process.

2. Face Resistance to Change: Resistance to change can be a significant challenge when implementing innovations. Involve the team in the innovation process from the beginning and clearly communicate the benefits of the changes. Provide training and support to help team members adapt to new approaches.

3. Ensure Adequate Resources: Innovation requires resources, including time, money and people. Make sure you have the resources you need to support your innovation efforts. This may include investments in technology, training and team development.

4. Foster an Innovative Mindset: Promote an innovative mindset in your organization, encouraging creativity and the search for continuous improvements. Recognize and reward innovation and create an environment where creativity is valued and encouraged.

Examples of Transformative Innovation

1. Tesla and the Electric Vehicle Revolution: Tesla is an example of transformative innovation in the automotive sector. The company revolutionized the electric vehicle market with its high-performance cars and innovative design. In addition to creating desirable electric vehicles, Tesla has also innovated its sales and service approach, using its own stores and software updates via the internet.

2. Netflix and the Disruption of Entertainment: Netflix transformed the entertainment industry by transforming from a DVD rental service to a global streaming platform. The company has not only innovated in the way content is distributed, but also in the production of original content. Netflix's innovative approach has changed the way people consume entertainment and set new standards in the industry.

3. SpaceX and Private Space Exploration: SpaceX, founded by Elon Musk, is an example of innovation in the aerospace sector. The company has introduced advanced technologies such as reusable rockets that have significantly reduced the cost of space missions. Musk's vision to make space exploration more accessible and sustainable is shaping the future of the industry.

The Power of Innovation and Creativity

Innovation and creativity are essential to outperform the

competition and achieve success. By cultivating a creative mindset and applying innovation strategically, you can turn challenges into opportunities and create a significant impact in your industry.

In this chapter, we explore the importance of innovation and creativity, how to develop and apply them in your business. Remember that innovation is not a one-off event, but an ongoing process of exploration and improvement. By adopting an innovative and creative approach, you will be better prepared to face challenges and seize opportunities that arise on your journey to success.

By the end of this chapter, I hope you have a clearer understanding of how innovation and creativity can be used to achieve your goals and outperform your competition. Adopt these practices in your life and career, and see how they can transform your approach and boost your success.

CHAPTER 8: NETWORKING STRATEGIES: BUILDING VALUABLE RELATIONSHIPS FOR SUCCESS

In the world of business and entrepreneurship, networking is an essential skill that can open doors and create valuable opportunities. Building and maintaining strong relationships can be the key to success, providing access to resources, advice, partnerships and even clients. In this chapter, we'll explore effective strategies for networking, how to build valuable relationships, and how to utilize those connections to achieve your goals.

O Valor do Networking

Networking goes beyond exchanging business cards and making superficial contacts. It's about building genuine, mutually beneficial relationships that can contribute to your personal and professional growth. Here are some reasons why networking is key:

1. Access to Opportunities: Building a strong network can provide access to opportunities that may not be available otherwise. This includes business opportunities, partnerships, investments and even new jobs. Often, the best opportunities arise through personal and professional connections.

2. Exchange of Knowledge and Ideas: Networking allows the exchange of knowledge and ideas with people from different areas and experiences. These interactions can offer new insights and perspectives, helping you solve problems and generate new ideas. Diversity of thoughts and experiences can enrich your understanding and approaches.

3. Support and Mentoring: Having a network also means having access to mentors and advisors who can offer guidance and support. These individuals can provide valuable advice, share their experiences, and help guide your career path. Mentoring is a crucial part of personal and professional development.

4. Development of Partnerships and Collaborations: Networking can lead to the formation of partnerships and collaborations that benefit both parties. Whether forming a joint venture, collaborating on projects or establishing strategic alliances, these partnerships can expand your ability to achieve goals and create new opportunities.

Strategies for Effective Networking

For networking to be truly effective, it is necessary to adopt strategies that help build and maintain valuable relationships. Here are some tips to improve your networking skills:

1. Define Your Networking Goals: Before you start building your network, clearly define what you want to achieve. Your goals may include finding new clients, pursuing business opportunities, finding mentors, or expanding your knowledge. Having clear goals will help guide your networking activities and measure your success.

2. Attend Events and Conferences: Events and conferences are excellent opportunities to meet new people and expand your network. Attend events relevant to your industry or area of interest and be prepared to engage and interact with other attendees. Take opportunities to introduce yourself and start conversations.

3. Use Online Networking Platforms: Online networking platforms, like LinkedIn, are powerful tools for building and maintaining professional relationships. Create a complete and updated profile, connect with relevant people and participate in groups and discussions. Use these platforms to share your knowledge and interact with other professionals.

4. Be Genuine and Authentic: When engaging in networking, it is important to be genuine and authentic. Show genuine interest in the people you are talking to and avoid superficial or purely transactional approaches. Solid relationships are built on trust and authenticity.

5. Offer Value and Help: Networking is a two-way street. Instead of just focusing on what you can gain, consider how you can provide value and help others. Share your experiences, offer advice, and be willing to help when possible. This approach creates a solid foundation for long-lasting and beneficial relationships.

6. Maintain Regular Contact: Building a network of contacts is just the beginning; It is equally important to maintain regular contact with your contacts. Send updates on your progress, share relevant information, and make an effort to keep the relationship active. Maintaining ongoing communication helps strengthen the connection and keep your network engaged.

7. Develop Communication Skills: Effective communication skills are crucial for networking. Learn to present yourself clearly and concisely, ask relevant questions, and listen actively. The ability to communicate your ideas and listen to others effectively can significantly improve the quality of your interactions.

8. Follow and Thank: After a meeting or networking event, it's important to follow up and thank your new contacts. Send a thank you email or follow-up message to express your appreciation for the conversation and to reinforce your connection. This demonstrates professionalism and helps keep the relationship positive.

Overcoming Networking Challenges

Although networking is a powerful tool, there can be challenges when building and maintaining a network of contacts. Here are some strategies for overcoming these challenges:

1. Overcome Shyness and Anxiety: If you are shy or experience anxiety in social situations, it can be difficult to start and maintain conversations. Prepare before events, practice your communication skills, and set small goals to interact with a specific number of people. Over time, you will gain confidence and feel more at ease.

2. Dealing with Rejection and Lack of Response: Not all contacts will be receptive or interested in building a relationship. It's important to deal with rejection constructively and move on. Don't be discouraged by the lack of response and continue to engage with other potential contacts.

3. Manage Time and Priorities: Networking can require a significant investment of time and effort. To manage your time and priorities, establish an action plan and define which events and activities are most relevant to your goals. Balance networking with other responsibilities and commitments.

4. Avoid Overly Commercial Approaches: Avoid approaching networking with an overly commercial or transactional mindset. Focusing only on obtaining benefits for yourself can be perceived as opportunistic. Instead, focus on building genuine relationships and offering value to others.

Examples of Successful Networking

1. Richard Branson and the Construction of the Virgin Group: Richard Branson is a notable example of how networking can contribute to business success. Branson used his networking skills to build a wide network of contacts and partnerships that helped expand the Virgin Group. His authentic and approachable networking style was instrumental in establishing long-term relationships and business opportunities.

2. Oprah Winfrey and Her Influential Connections: Oprah Winfrey is known for her ability to build and maintain valuable relationships. Her approach to networking includes building genuine connections with influential people and creating a support network. Winfrey has used these connections to boost her career and expand her business and social initiatives.

3. Elon Musk and His Contacts in the Technology Industry: Elon Musk is an example of how networking can drive innovation and success. Musk has built a network of influential contacts in the technology and aerospace industry, who have played an important role in the development of companies like Tesla and SpaceX. Their connections helped secure investments, partnerships and strategic support.

The Power of Networking for Success

Networking is a powerful tool for building valuable relationships and achieving success. By adopting effective networking strategies, you can create opportunities, exchange knowledge, obtain support and develop partnerships that can boost your career and ventures.

In this chapter, we explore the importance of networking, strategies for building it effectively, and how to overcome common challenges. Remember that networking is an ongoing process and that building strong relationships takes time, effort and authenticity. By cultivating a valuable network and maintaining those connections, you will be better prepared to face challenges, seize opportunities, and achieve your goals.

Adopt the networking practices discussed in this chapter and see how they can transform your approach and contribute to your success. With a solid network of contacts, you will have the support and resources you need to face challenges and achieve your goals effectively.

CHAPTER 9: THE ART OF DECISION MAKING: HOW TO MAKE STRATEGIC AND EFFECTIVE CHOICES

Making decisions is a fundamental part of business and entrepreneurial life. Each decision can profoundly impact the trajectory and success of a business or project. However, decision making can often be challenging due to the complexity and uncertainties involved. In this chapter, we will explore the art of decision making, discussing methods and strategies for making strategic and effective choices, and analyzing examples of how great leaders and entrepreneurs made decisions that shaped their success trajectories.

The Importance of Decision Making

Making decisions is a critical skill that can determine the success or failure of an enterprise. Right decisions can lead to growth, innovation and success, while wrong decisions can result in obstacles and failures. Here are some reasons why decision making is crucial:

1. Direction and Focus: Well-informed decisions help define the direction and focus of a business. They guide the allocation of resources, the development of strategies and the definition of goals. A clear, strategic decision can align the team and efforts around common goals.

2. Troubleshooting: Making effective decisions is essential for solving problems and facing challenges. Each problem or obstacle requires a decision about the best approach to overcome it. The ability to evaluate options and choose the best solution is crucial to successful problem solving.

3. Taking advantage of opportunities: Quick, well-informed decisions can help you capitalize on business and growth opportunities. In a competitive environment, the ability to make strategic decisions quickly can mean the difference between seizing an opportunity and losing a competitive advantage.

4. Risk Management: Effective decisions involve risk assessment and management. Making informed decisions allows you to anticipate and mitigate risks, minimizing negative impacts and maximizing the chances of success. Risk management is an essential part of the decision-making process.

Methods for Making Effective Decisions

There are several methods and approaches to making decisions effectively. Here are some of the key techniques that can help improve the decision-making process:

1. SWOT Analysis (Strengths, Weaknesses, Opportunities and Threats): SWOT analysis is a useful tool for evaluating the position of a business and identifying internal and external factors that may influence the decision. By analyzing strengths, weaknesses, opportunities and threats, you can get a clear picture of the aspects to consider and make a more informed decision.

2. Data-Driven Decision Making: Data-driven decisions involve collecting and analyzing relevant information to guide the choice. Using data and analytics to inform your decisions can increase accuracy and effectiveness by reducing reliance on intuition or guesswork.

3. Multiple Criteria Decision Method: This method involves evaluating several options based on specific criteria. By assigning weights to different criteria and evaluating how each option meets those criteria, you can compare alternatives in a structured way and identify the best choice.

4. Cost-Benefit Analysis: Cost-benefit analysis involves comparing the costs and benefits of different options to determine which one offers the best return on investment. Evaluating the costs associated with each option and the expected benefits helps you make a sound financial decision.

5. 5 Whys Method: The 5 Whys method is a simple technique for identifying the root cause of a problem and making informed decisions about the solution. By repeatedly questioning the reason behind a problem, you can come to a deeper understanding and develop an effective solution.

6. Consult Experts and Mentors: Seeking input from experts and mentors can provide a valuable outside perspective. Consulting people with experience and knowledge in the field can help clarify options and provide additional insights that may influence your decision.

Strategies for Making Decisions in Complex Situations

Making decisions in complex situations can be especially challenging. Here are some strategies for facing these challenges and making effective decisions:

1. Collect Relevant Information: In complex situations, it is crucial to gather as much relevant information as possible. Researching and understanding all aspects of the problem or opportunity can provide a solid basis for decision making. Be sure to consider all available variables and data.

2. **Evaluate Alternatives:** Develop and evaluate different alternatives before making a decision. Exploring several options and considering the pros and cons of each can help identify the best solution. Don't limit yourself to the first option that comes up; consider different approaches to find the most effective one.

3. **Consider the Long-Term Impact:** Evaluate the impact of your decisions not only in the short term, but also in the long term. Consider how the decision will affect the future of the business, team and long-term goals. Making decisions with a long-term vision can help avoid future problems and ensure sustainability.

4. **Implement a Structured Decision Process:** Establish a structured decision process to deal with complex situations. This may include steps such as analyzing information, discussing with the team, evaluating alternatives, and reviewing implications. A structured process helps ensure that all considerations are addressed and the decision is well-informed.

5. **Be Prepared for Adjustments:** Sometimes, even with careful planning, circumstances can change and require adjustments. Be prepared to review and adjust your decision as necessary. Flexibility and a willingness to adapt to change are important for dealing with complexity and uncertainty.

Examples of Successful Decision Making

1. Jeff Bezos and the Decision to Invest in Amazon Web Services (AWS): Jeff Bezos, founder of Amazon, made a crucial strategic decision by investing in Amazon Web Services (AWS). At the time, Amazon was known primarily as an online retailer, but Bezos saw an opportunity in the growing demand for cloud computing services. The investment in AWS proved to be a huge success and helped diversify and expand Amazon's business.

2. Indra Nooyi and the Transformation of PepsiCo: Indra Nooyi, former CEO of PepsiCo, made important strategic decisions to transform the company. She led the shift to healthier products and the acquisition of companies like Tropicana and Quaker Oats. These decisions helped PepsiCo adapt to changing consumer preferences and strengthen its market position.

3. Elon Musk and the Decision to Focus on Electric Vehicles at Tesla: Elon Musk made the strategic decision to focus on electric vehicles at Tesla, despite the challenges and risks involved. This decision was fundamental in positioning Tesla as a leader in the electric car sector and contributing to change in the automotive market. Musk has taken significant risks and made investments in technology and innovation that have paid dividends in the long term.

Overcoming Challenges in Decision Making

Making decisions can involve challenges and risks. Here are some strategies for overcoming these challenges and making more effective decisions:

1. Manage Anxiety and Fear: Fear and anxiety can negatively influence decision making. Learn to manage these emotions and make decisions based on data and information instead of letting yourself be carried away by fear. Stress management and decision-making techniques can help maintain clarity and confidence.

2. Dealing with Incomplete Information: Sometimes there may be a lack of complete information when making decisions. In such cases, it is important to do the best you can with the information available and consider the risks involved. Evaluate incomplete information and make decisions based on a careful analysis of what you know.

3. Avoid Analysis Standstill: Excessive analysis can lead to analysis paralysis, where decision-making is delayed due to the search for more information. Set a deadline for making a decision and trust your analysis process. The ability to make decisions in a timely manner is crucial to success.

4. Accept and Learn from Mistakes: Not all decisions will be perfect, and it is important to accept and learn from mistakes. Analyze what went wrong, adjust your approach, and use the experience to improve your decision-making skills in the future. Continuous learning is an essential part of the decision-making process.

The Art of Decision Making

Making effective decisions is an essential skill for achieving success in any endeavor. Understanding methods and strategies for making informed decisions, overcoming challenges, and learning from experience can help you hone your skills and achieve your goals.

In this chapter, we explore the importance of decision making, effective methods, and strategies for facing challenges. Remember that decision-making is an ongoing process and the ability to evaluate options, manage risks and learn from mistakes is crucial to success.

Adopt the practices discussed in this chapter and see how they can improve your approach to decision making. With a strategic mindset and improved skills, you will be better prepared to face challenges, seize opportunities and achieve your goals effectively.

CHAPTER 10: INNOVATION AND CREATIVITY: CULTIVATING THE MINDSET THAT DRIVES SUCCESS

In today's competitive world, innovation and creativity are more important than ever. Companies that thrive are those that can think outside the box, challenge the status quo and create new, impactful solutions. In this chapter, we'll explore how to cultivate an innovative and creative mindset, discuss strategies for stimulating innovation, and examine examples of how creativity can drive success.

The Role of Innovation and Creativity in Success

Innovation and creativity are essential drivers of growth and success. They allow companies and entrepreneurs to stand out in a saturated market, create differentiated products and services and adapt to changing consumer needs and preferences. Here are some reasons why innovation and creativity are crucial:

1. Market Differentiation: In a highly competitive environment, innovation helps differentiate your brand and products from the competition. Creating something unique and valuable can attract customers and create a competitive advantage. Differentiation is key to building a strong brand identity and establishing a leading position in the market.

2. Troubleshooting: Creativity is a powerful tool for solving complex problems and finding effective solutions. Instead of following traditional approaches, thinking creatively can lead to new ways of facing challenges and overcoming obstacles. The ability to find innovative solutions can improve efficiency and effectiveness.

3. Adaptation to Changes: The market and consumer needs are constantly evolving. Innovation allows you to adapt to these changes and stay relevant. By being willing to try new ideas and approaches, you can anticipate trends and quickly adjust to new demands.

4. Stimulating Growth: Innovation can drive growth and expansion. New products, services and business models can open up new opportunities and markets. Creativity allows you to explore new possibilities and expand your reach, contributing to sustainable growth.

Strategies for Cultivating Innovation and Creativity

Cultivating an innovative and creative mindset requires effort and consistent practices. Here are some strategies to stimulate innovation and foster creativity:

1. Promote an Innovative Work Environment: Creating a work environment that encourages innovation is key to cultivating creativity. This may include allowing experimentation, encouraging the exchange of ideas, and rewarding creativity. An environment that values innovation and creativity can encourage employees to think differently and contribute new ideas.

2. Encourage Diversity of Thought: Diversity of thoughts and perspectives is an important driver for innovation. Bring people with different backgrounds, experiences and skills onto your team. Diversity encourages the exchange of ideas and collaboration, leading to more creative and innovative solutions.

3. Adopt a Continuous Learning Mindset: Innovation is linked to continuous learning. Be open to new ideas and information and constantly seek to improve your skills and knowledge. Take courses, read books, and be aware of trends and innovations in your area. Constant learning keeps your mind sharp and ready for new approaches.

4. Encourage Experimentation and Failure: Don't be afraid to experiment and take risks. Innovation often involves trial and error, and failure is a natural part of the process. Encourage experimentation and see failure as a learning opportunity. The ability to learn from mistakes and adjust your approaches is essential for innovative success.

5. Create a Space for Ideas: Dedicate time and resources to generating and developing new ideas. This could include brainstorming sessions, hackathons or innovation workshops. Provide a space where creativity can flourish and where ideas can be explored and refined.

6. Involve Customers in the Innovation Process: Customers can be a valuable source of ideas and feedback. Involve them in the innovation process through surveys, focus groups and product testing. Understanding your customers' needs and wants can help you direct your innovation efforts and create solutions that better meet their expectations.

7. Use Innovative Technologies and Tools: Technology can be a great ally in innovation. Use tools and platforms that facilitate the creation, development and implementation of new ideas. From design software to data analysis tools, technology can support and accelerate the innovative process.

Examples of Innovation and Creativity in the Business World

1. Apple and the Product Design Revolution: Apple is known for its innovation and creativity in product design. The introduction of the iPhone, for example, revolutionized the mobile phone industry with its elegant design and advanced features. Apple invested in research and development to create a product that not only met consumers' needs but also set new standards for the industry.

2. Google and Innovation in the Workplace: Google is famous for its innovative work environment and practices that encourage creativity. Google gives employees time to work on personal projects and encourages collaboration and sharing ideas. This stimulating environment contributes to the development of innovative products and services, such as Google Maps and Google Drive.

3. Tesla and the Electric Vehicle Revolution: Tesla, under the leadership of Elon Musk, has been an innovative force in the automotive sector. The company challenged the norm by producing high-performance electric vehicles and creating a global charging infrastructure. Musk's vision and Tesla's creative approach have helped accelerate the adoption of electric vehicles and promote sustainability.

4. Airbnb and the Reinvention of Hospitality: Airbnb revolutionized the hospitality industry by creating a platform that connects hosts and travelers. The company innovated by offering an alternative to traditional hotels and creating a more personalized and accessible experience. Airbnb's creative approach has helped transform the lodging market and expand options for consumers.

Overcoming Barriers to Innovation

Although innovation is essential, there are several barriers that can hinder the creative process. Here are some strategies for overcoming these barriers and fostering a culture of innovation:

1. Overcome the Fear of Failure: Fear of failure can inhibit creativity and the willingness to try new ideas. Encourage a mindset where failure is seen as an opportunity to learn and grow. Foster an environment where employees feel safe to take risks and experiment without fear of reprimand.

2. Dealing with Resistance to Change: Resistance to change is a common barrier to innovation. To overcome this resistance, clearly communicate the benefits of innovation and involve employees in the change process. Provide training and support to help ease the transition and adoption of new ideas.

3. Manage Resources and Priorities: Innovation can require significant investments of time and resources. Manage your priorities and allocate adequate resources to support innovative initiatives. Balance everyday demands with efforts to develop and implement new ideas.

4. Maintain Customer Focus: Sometimes companies can stray from focusing on customer needs when pursuing innovation. Keep the customer at the center of the innovation process and ensure that your ideas and products meet their expectations. Conduct research and collect feedback to guide your innovative initiatives.

Cultivating an Innovative Mindset

Cultivating an innovative and creative mindset is essential for success in a competitive and constantly changing market. By fostering an environment that values creativity, encouraging diversity of thought, and taking an open approach to learning and experimentation, you can stimulate innovation and achieve impactful results.

In this chapter, we explore strategies for cultivating innovation, overcoming barriers, and using successful examples to inspire and guide your own creative initiatives. By applying these practices and adopting an innovation mindset, you will be better prepared to face challenges, explore new opportunities and achieve success in your endeavors.

Innovation and creativity are powerful forces that can transform your business and drive its growth. Embrace these practices, stay open to new ideas, and continue looking for ways to improve and evolve. With an innovative mindset, you will be ready to face the future and achieve success in a meaningful and impactful way.

CHAPTER 11: NETWORKING AND BUILDING RELATIONSHIPS: THE POWER OF CONNECTIONS IN ENTREPRENEURIAL SUCCESS

In the business world, success is not achieved through technical skills and knowledge alone. Relationship building and networking are crucial components that can open doors, provide support, and create opportunities for growth and innovation. In this chapter, we will explore the critical role of networking and relationship building in entrepreneurial success, discuss strategies for building and maintaining an effective network, and analyze examples of how powerful connections have contributed to the success of great entrepreneurs.

The Value of Networking and Connections

Networking is more than just collecting business cards or making superficial contacts. It's about building meaningful, lasting relationships that can benefit both parties. Here are some ways networking and relationship building can impact your success:

1. Business Opportunities: A strong network can provide access to new business opportunities and partnerships. Connecting with influential and well-connected people can open doors to collaborations, investments and new markets. Opportunities often arise through personal and professional connections.

2. Access to Knowledge and Experience: Relationships with mentors, peers, and experts can provide valuable insights and strategic guidance. Exchanging ideas and experiences can help you solve problems, improve your skills and expand your knowledge. The experience of others can provide perspective that you may not have considered.

3. Support and Motivation: Building a support network can be essential in challenging times. Having people to trust and who offer moral and professional support can be a great motivator. Support from peers and mentors can help overcome obstacles and keep motivation high.

4. Reputation and Credibility: The way you are perceived by your contacts can influence your reputation and credibility. Building strong relationships and being known for your integrity and competence can increase your reputation in the industry. The trust and respect you build with your contacts can open doors and create opportunities.

5. Resource and Information Sharing: A network of contacts can be a valuable source of resources and information. Exchanging knowledge about market trends, business opportunities and useful resources can be beneficial. Sharing and receiving information within your network can increase your ability to make informed decisions.

Strategies for Building and Maintaining an Effective Network

Building and maintaining an effective network of contacts requires effort and strategy. Here are some strategies for developing meaningful, lasting relationships:

1. Identify Your Networking Goals: Before you start building your network, clearly define your goals. Ask yourself what you hope to achieve through networking. It could be finding mentors, expanding your business opportunities, or learning from other professionals. Having clear objectives will help you direct your efforts and build relationships that align with your goals.

2. Attend Events and Conferences: Attending industry events, conferences and trade shows is an effective way to connect with others in your area of interest. These events provide opportunities to meet influential people, learn about current trends, and expand your network. Be prepared to introduce yourself, ask questions, and engage in meaningful conversations.

3. Use Social Media Strategically: Social media is a powerful tool for networking. Platforms like LinkedIn, Twitter and Facebook allow you to connect with professionals from all over the world. Use these platforms to share your achievements, interact with other professionals and engage in relevant discussions. Keep an up-to-date profile and actively participate in conversations in your field.

4. Build Long-Term Relationships: Networking should not just be about making new contacts, but also about maintaining existing relationships. Keep in regular contact with your connections, offer support when needed, and stay up to date with their activities. Lasting relationships are built on trust and mutual respect.

5. Offer Value and Help Others: An effective approach to networking is to offer value and help others. Be generous with your time, knowledge and resources. By helping others and offering support, you create an environment of reciprocity and lay a solid foundation for future relationships. People tend to remember and value those who were useful to them.

6. Seek Mentors and Advisors: Finding mentors and advisors can be an effective way to build a support network. Mentors offer valuable guidance, feedback, and advice that can help you grow professionally. Look for people with experience and knowledge in your field who are willing to share their wisdom and help you achieve your goals.

7. Participate in Professional Groups and Associations: Joining professional groups and associations can provide opportunities to build meaningful connections with people who share similar interests and goals. These groups provide a platform for networking, learning and collaboration. Attend meetings, events and activities to maximize your participation.

8. Maintain an Authentic Approach: Authenticity is key to building genuine relationships. Be yourself and avoid trying to impress or show yourself as something you are not. Authentic relationships are based on sincerity and trust, and tend to be more lasting and valuable.

Examples of Networking and Building Relationships in the Business World

1. Richard Branson and the Virgin Network: Richard Branson, founder of the Virgin Group, is known for his ability to build a network of influential contacts. Branson used his network to expand Virgin's business into different sectors, including music, aviation and telecommunications. His connections helped create business opportunities and promote the Virgin brand.

2. Oprah Winfrey and Her Strategic Partnerships: Oprah Winfrey has built a successful career not only on her communication skills, but also on her ability to build strategic relationships. His partnerships with other celebrities and influencers have contributed to the success of his television show and the growth of his personal brand.

3. Elon Musk and Collaboration with Other Entrepreneurs: Elon Musk is known for his collaborations and partnerships with other entrepreneurs and companies. His connections with people like Larry Page and Sergey Brin, founders of Google, helped drive initiatives like the SolarCity project and SpaceX. Strategic partnerships have been a key part of its success.

4. Sheryl Sandberg and the Facebook Leadership Network: Sheryl Sandberg, COO of Facebook, has built a significant network throughout her career. His connections with business and political leaders have helped position Facebook as one of the most influential companies in the world. Sandberg also used her network to promote her leadership and female empowerment initiatives.

Overcoming Networking Challenges

While networking is essential, it can present challenges. Here are some strategies for overcoming obstacles and building an effective network:

1. Dealing with Shyness or Anxiety: If you are shy or anxious at networking events, practice techniques to overcome these feelings. Prepare in advance, set clear goals for the event, and use coping strategies to manage anxiety. Practice and preparation can help build your confidence.

2. Maintain Quality over Quantity: Don't just focus on increasing the number of contacts. Instead, focus on building quality relationships with people who can truly contribute to your goals.

Deep, meaningful relationships are more valuable than a lot of superficial connections.

3. Manage Time and Priorities: Building and maintaining a network can require a significant investment of time. Manage your priorities and find a balance between networking and other activities. Set a plan to connect with your network regularly and allocate time for important events and interactions.

4. Navigate Complex Relationships: Not all relationships will be simple or straightforward. Some connections may involve complex dynamics or challenges. Maintain a professional approach and treat everyone with respect, even in difficult situations. The ability to deal with complex relationships can strengthen your network and increase its effectiveness.

The Power of Connections in Entrepreneurial Success

Networking and building relationships are crucial components of entrepreneurial success. Building and maintaining an effective network can provide opportunities, access to knowledge, support and a solid reputation. By adopting strategies to develop meaningful and authentic connections, you can expand your reach and achieve your goals more effectively.

In this chapter, we discuss the value of networking, strategies for building and maintaining an effective network, and examples of how powerful connections have contributed to the success of great entrepreneurs. By applying these practices and focusing on building authentic, valuable relationships, you will be better prepared to seize opportunities and achieve success in your endeavors.

Networking is a powerful tool that can transform your career and your business. Invest time and effort in building your network and take advantage of the opportunities that arise through these connections. With a strategic approach and an open mindset, you will be ready to face the challenges and seize the opportunities that the future holds.

CHAPTER 12: TIME MANAGEMENT AND PRODUCTIVITY: MAXIMIZING THE ENJOYMENT OF YOUR DAY

Time management and productivity are crucial aspects for any successful entrepreneur. In a world where demands are constant and challenges are unpredictable, the ability to manage your time effectively can make all the difference between success and failure. In this chapter, we'll explore techniques and strategies to improve your time management, increase productivity, and create a healthy work-life balance.

The Importance of Time Management

Managing your time effectively is essential to achieving your goals and staying productive. Here are some reasons why time management is crucial:

1. Increases Productivity: Good time management allows you to focus on important tasks and maximize your efficiency. By planning and prioritizing your activities, you can accomplish more in less time and achieve better results.

2. Reduces Stress: Lack of organization and poor time management can lead to stress and overload. By establishing a clear plan and meeting deadlines, you reduce pressure and create a calmer work environment.

3. Improves Quality of Work: When you manage your time effectively, you can devote more time and attention to tasks, which results in higher quality work. Avoiding procrastination and multitasking can improve accuracy and efficiency.

4. Provides More Time for Personal Activities: Effective time management not only benefits your work, but also gives you more time for your personal activities and leisure. Finding a balance between work and personal life is essential for overall well-being and satisfaction.

Strategies for Managing Time Effectively

Here are some proven strategies to improve your time management and increase your productivity:

1. Set Clear and Realistic Goals: Set clear and specific goals for what you want to achieve. Break your goals into smaller, more manageable steps. This makes it easier to see progress and stay focused.

2. Prioritize Tasks with the Eisenhower Matrix: The Eisenhower Matrix is a useful tool for prioritizing tasks based on their urgency and importance. Sort your tasks into four categories: urgent and important, important, urgent, and neither urgent nor important. Focus on the tasks that are urgent and important and plan how to handle the other categories.

3. Use the Pomodoro Technique: The Pomodoro Technique is a popular approach to increasing productivity. Work on a task for 25 minutes, then take a 5-minute break. After four "pomodoros," take a longer break of 15 to 30 minutes. This method helps you stay focused and avoid fatigue.

4. Create a Daily and Weekly Plan: Develop a daily and weekly plan to organize your tasks and commitments. Include a list of priority tasks and schedule blocks of time to complete each one. Review and adjust your plan regularly to reflect changing priorities and progress.

5. Avoid Procrastination: Procrastination can be a significant obstacle to productivity. Identify the causes of procrastination and adopt strategies to overcome it, such as setting short deadlines, eliminating distractions, and using the "start small" technique to begin difficult tasks.

6. Delegate Tasks: Don't try to do everything alone. Delegate tasks when possible and trust your team's capabilities. Delegating not only frees up your time for more important activities, but also develops your employees' skills and responsibility.

7. Use Productivity Tools and Technologies: Take advantage of productivity tools and apps to manage your time and tasks. Tools like digital calendars, to-do list apps, and project management platforms can help you stay organized and efficient.

8. Set Limits and Maintain a Balance: Set clear boundaries between work and personal life. Avoid working overtime and reserve time for personal activities and rest. Maintaining a healthy balance is essential for longevity and job satisfaction.

9. Assess and Adjust Regularly: Regularly evaluate how you are managing your time and adjust your strategies as needed. Self-evaluation and reflection on what is working and what needs improvement can help optimize your approach.

Examples of Effective Time Management

1. Tim Ferriss and the Concept of "4-Hour Work": Tim Ferriss, author of the book "The 4-Hour Work," is known for his innovative approaches to time management and productivity. Ferriss advocates eliminating unnecessary tasks and automating processes to maximize efficiency. His concept of the "4-hour job" is based on the idea that you can achieve significant results with fewer hours of work by focusing on what's most important.

2. Elon Musk and Time Management in Blocks: Elon Musk, CEO of Tesla and SpaceX, is known for his rigorous approach to time management. Musk divides his day into 5-minute blocks and allocates each block to a specific task. This detailed approach allows him to maximize his time and stay focused on multiple complex projects.

3. Marie Kondo and the Organization of the Workplace: Marie Kondo, author of the book "The Magic of Tidying Up", is known for her approach to organizing and managing space. Kondo suggests that an organized work environment can increase productivity and reduce stress. Applying organizational principles to the workplace can help improve efficiency and mental clarity.

4. Steve Jobs and Focus on Priorities: Steve Jobs, co-founder of Apple, was known for his ability to focus on a few essential priorities. Jobs believed in simplifying and focusing on what really matters, avoiding distractions and maintaining clarity about the main goals and objectives. His approach helped Apple stand out with innovative, high-quality products.

Overcoming Time Management Challenges

Time management can present challenges, and overcoming these obstacles is critical to maintaining productivity. Here are some tips for dealing with common challenges:

1. Dealing with Distractions: Distractions are a common challenge to productivity. Identify your main sources of distraction and adopt strategies to minimize them. This can include creating an interruption-free work environment, using distraction-blocking apps, and setting specific times to check emails and social media.

2. Manage Unexpected Outages: Unexpected interruptions can divert your attention and affect your productivity. Have a plan for dealing with these interruptions, such as creating a priority task list and allocating specific time to resolve urgent issues. Maintain flexibility in your plan to adjust to changes.

3. Coping with Work Overload: Work overload can occur when you have too many tasks to complete in a short period of time. Learn to identify signs of overload and adopt strategies to deal with it, such as prioritizing tasks, delegating responsibilities and practicing stress management techniques.

4. Maintain Motivation: Maintaining motivation over time can be challenging. Set clear goals and celebrate small achievements along the way. Engage in activities that inspire you and maintain a positive mindset to overcome obstacles and stay motivated.

Maximizing Time and Productivity

Managing time and increasing productivity are essential skills for any entrepreneur who wants to achieve success. By applying effective strategies to organize your time, prioritize tasks, and maintain a healthy work-life balance, you can maximize your day and achieve your goals more efficiently.

In this chapter, we explore the importance of time management, techniques and strategies for improving productivity, examples of success, and common challenges. By adopting these practices and adjusting your approach as needed, you will be better prepared to face challenges and seize opportunities as they arise.

Effective time management is not just a skill, but an ongoing commitment to achieving meaningful results and maintaining a healthy balance. With careful planning and a focused mindset, you can optimize your time and maximize your success in all aspects of your life.

CHAPTER 13: RESILIENCE AND OVERCOMING: HOW TO FACE ADVERSITY AND STAY FOCUSED

The entrepreneurial journey is full of challenges and adversities. Resilience – the ability to recover and adapt in the face of difficulties – is a crucial skill for any successful entrepreneur. In this chapter, we'll explore the importance of resilience, how to develop this skill, and examples of how overcoming adversity can lead to success. We will discuss practical strategies for facing challenges and staying focused, even when circumstances are difficult.

The Importance of Resilience in Entrepreneurship

Resilience is the ability to face, overcome and recover from adverse situations. In the context of entrepreneurship, resilience is essential for several reasons:

1. Facing Uncertainties: The business world is unpredictable and constantly changing. Entrepreneurs face uncertainties related to the market, finances and competition. Resilience allows you to adapt and keep moving forward, even when the situation is uncertain and challenging.

2. Overcoming Failures: Failures are an inevitable part of the entrepreneurial journey. Being resilient means learning from mistakes, adjusting your approach, and keeping trying. Instead of being discouraged by failures, you see them as opportunities to learn and grow.

3. Maintain Motivation: Maintaining motivation during difficult times can be a challenge. Resilience helps you stay focused on your goals and find ways to stay motivated, even when things don't go as planned.

4. Adapt to Changes: Unexpected changes can occur at any time. Being resilient means being flexible and able to adapt quickly to new circumstances. This is essential to adjust your strategies and continue moving towards success.

5. Build a Positive Mindset: Resilience is related to a positive mindset and the ability to maintain perspective. Instead of focusing on problems, you focus on solutions and opportunities. This contributes to a healthier and more productive mental state.

Strategies for Developing Resilience

Developing resilience is an ongoing process that involves practice and adapting to challenges. Here are some strategies to strengthen your resilience:

1. Develop a Growth Mindset: Adopt a growth mindset, which is the belief that your skills and capabilities can be developed with effort and practice. View challenges and failures as opportunities to learn and grow rather than as insurmountable obstacles.

2. Establish Clear and Realistic Objectives: Set clear and realistic goals for your entrepreneurial journey. Having specific goals helps you stay focused and motivated, even in difficult times. Break your goals into smaller steps and achieve them progressively.

3. Cultivate a Support System: Build a support network made up of mentors, fellow entrepreneurs, friends and family. Having a support system can provide advice, encouragement, and emotional support during challenging times. Don't hesitate to seek help when you need it.

4. Practice Self-Care: Take care of your physical and mental health to strengthen your resilience. This includes maintaining a balanced diet, exercising regularly and ensuring adequate sleep. Self-care is essential to maintaining your energy and well-being.

5. Develop Problem Solving Skills: The ability to solve problems effectively is an important part of resilience. Work to improve your problem-solving skills by learning to analyze situations, identify solutions, and make informed decisions.

6. Maintain a Positive Outlook: Develop the ability to see the positive side of situations, even when facing challenges. Maintaining a positive outlook helps reduce stress and maintain motivation. Practice gratitude and focus on achievements and progress rather than obstacles.

7. Learn to Manage Stress: Adopt stress management techniques, such as meditation, deep breathing and practicing relaxing activities. Managing stress effectively helps you maintain mental clarity and resilience in times of pressure.

8. Be Flexible and Adaptable: Flexibility is an essential part of resilience. Be willing to adjust your strategies and approaches as needed. The ability to adapt to new circumstances and changes is crucial to overcoming challenges.

Examples of Resilience in the Business World

1. Steve Jobs and the Return to Apple: Steve Jobs faced a series of challenges and failures throughout his career, including his dismissal from Apple in 1985. However, he didn't let that discourage him. Jobs continued to innovate and eventually returned to Apple, where he led the company to monumental success with revolutionary products like the iPhone and iPad. His resilience and vision were instrumental in transforming Apple into one of the most valuable companies in the world.

2. J.K. Rowling and the Publication of Harry Potter: J.K. Rowling faced countless rejections before finding a publisher for the first book in the Harry Potter series. Instead of giving up, she continued to believe in her story and pursue opportunities. His perseverance resulted in the publication of one of the best-selling books of all time and the creation of a successful global franchise.

3. Howard Schultz and the Transformation of Starbucks: Howard Schultz faced many challenges when trying to transform Starbucks from a small coffee chain into a global brand. It faced resistance, financial difficulties and changes in the market. However, his resilience and determination helped him overcome these obstacles and build Starbucks into one of the largest and most well-known coffee chains in the world.

4. Elon Musk and the Challenges of SpaceX: Elon Musk faced several challenges while building SpaceX, including failed launches and financial problems. Instead of giving in, Musk continued to invest and innovate. SpaceX's resilience has led to success with rocket recovery and the achievement of significant milestones in space exploration.

Strategies for Facing Adversity

Facing adversity is an inevitable part of entrepreneurship. Here are some strategies for dealing with these challenges effectively:

1. Face Problems Head-on: When facing a challenge, it is important to address it directly and not avoid the situation.

Identify the problem, analyze its causes and develop a plan to resolve the issue. Facing problems head on allows you to find solutions and move forward.

2. Adopt a Solving Approach: Focus on finding solutions rather than dwelling on problems. Develop a problem-solving approach, which involves identifying possible solutions, evaluating options, and implementing actions to overcome the challenge.

3. Maintain Calm and Mental Clarity: Staying calm during times of crisis is essential for making rational and effective decisions. Practice breathing and mindfulness techniques to help maintain mental clarity and deal with stress constructively.

4. Seek Feedback and Learning: Ask mentors, peers, and experts for feedback to gain new perspectives on how to tackle challenges. Learning from the experience of others can provide valuable insights and help you find effective solutions.

5. Maintain Persistence: Persistence is an essential quality for overcoming adversity. Even when challenges seem insurmountable, continue to work toward your goals. Persistence can lead to new opportunities and long-term success.

6. Reevaluate and Adjust Your Strategies: If one approach isn't working, reevaluate your strategies and adjust as needed. Flexibility is important to adapt to changes and find new ways to overcome challenges.

7. Celebrate Small Wins: Recognize and celebrate your small victories along the way. This helps you maintain motivation and recognize progress, even when facing significant challenges.

Strengthening Resilience for Success

Resilience and the ability to overcome adversity are fundamental to success in entrepreneurship. Developing resilience involves adopting a growth mindset, setting clear goals, cultivating a support system, and practicing self-care. Facing challenges effectively requires a problem-solving approach, the ability to remain calm and persistence.

In this chapter, we explore the importance of resilience, strategies for developing it, and examples of how overcoming adversity can lead to success. By strengthening your resilience and adopting strategies to face challenges, you will be better prepared to deal with difficulties and continue moving towards your goals.

Resilience is a skill that can be developed and improved over time. By practicing and applying these strategies, you will be creating a solid foundation to face the challenges of entrepreneurship and achieve long-term success.

CHAPTER 14: RESILIENCE AND ADAPTATION: OVERCOMING ADVERSITY AND CHANGE

In the business world, the ability to be resilient and adapt to change is critical to long-term success. The entrepreneurial journey is full of challenges, unforeseen events and rapid changes. Resilience and adaptability not only help you overcome these obstacles, but they also allow you to seize opportunities and continue to grow. In this chapter, we will explore the concept of resilience, strategies for developing this skill, and examples of how adaptation can lead to success.

The Concept of Resilience

Resilience is the ability to recover from adversity, overcome challenges and adjust to changes effectively. It is an essential quality for entrepreneurs, as the path to success is often marked by ups and downs. Resilience involves not only resisting difficulties, but also learning and growing from them. Here are some key aspects of resilience:

1. Acceptance of Reality: Being resilient starts with accepting reality. Instead of denying or fighting challenges, accept them as a natural part of the entrepreneurial journey. Recognizing reality helps to deal with the situation more effectively and find solutions.

2. Open-Minded and Flexible: Resilience requires an open and flexible mind. Be willing to consider new approaches and adjust your strategy as needed. The ability to change direction when circumstances change is crucial to adaptation and long-term success.

3. Self-efficacy and Confidence: Having a solid belief in your abilities and capabilities is fundamental to resilience. Self-efficacy, or confidence in your ability to overcome challenges, helps you maintain motivation and persist in the face of adversity.

4. Support Network: Having a solid support network can be a valuable resource during difficult times. Friends, family, mentors and colleagues can offer emotional and practical support. Building and maintaining strong relationships can provide a solid foundation during challenging times.

5. Continuous Learning: Resilience involves learning from experiences and applying that learning to improve. Analyze your failures and challenges, identify lessons, and use this information to make adjustments and improve your approach in the future.

Strategies for Developing Resilience

Developing resilience is an ongoing process that involves practicing and adapting strategies. Here are some effective strategies to strengthen your resilience:

1. Cultivate a Positive Mindset: Adopting a positive mindset helps you face challenges with optimism and confidence. Focus on opportunities instead of focusing on difficulties. Practice gratitude and recognize the small victories along the way.

2. Set Goals and Stay Focused: Set clear, realistic goals for yourself and stay focused on those goals. Having defined goals provides a sense of purpose and directs your efforts. Even in the face of adversity, staying focused on goals helps maintain motivation.

3. Develop Problem Solving Skills: Resilience involves the ability to solve problems creatively and effectively. Develop problem-solving skills and look for innovative solutions to the challenges you face. Continuous practice and application of problem-solving techniques can strengthen your resilience.

4. Take Care of Your Physical and Mental Health: Physical and mental health play a crucial role in resilience. Maintain an exercise routine, a balanced diet and good quality sleep. Additionally, practice stress management techniques such as meditation, deep breathing and mindfulness.

5. Face Your Fears and Challenges: Resilience is strengthened by facing your fears and challenges directly. Instead of avoiding difficult situations, face them head on and look for ways to overcome them. Gradual exposure to challenges can help build your confidence and resilience.

6. Build a Contingency Plan: Having a contingency plan helps you prepare for unexpected situations. Identify possible risks and develop strategies to deal with them. Having an action plan can reduce anxiety and provide a sense of control.

7. Maintain Adaptability: Adaptability is a fundamental part of resilience. Be willing to adjust your approach and learn from experience. The ability to quickly adapt to changes can help you face challenges more effectively.

Examples of Resilience and Adaptation in the Business World

1. Apple and the Replacement of Steve Jobs: When Steve Jobs left Apple in 1985, the company faced a challenging period. However, Apple restructured itself and adapted to new market conditions. Jobs' return in 1997 brought new vision and innovation, leading Apple to become one of the most valuable companies in the world.

2. Netflix and the Transition to Streaming: Netflix began as a DVD rental service, but quickly adapted to changing technology and increased demand for streaming. The company invested in technology and produced original content, becoming a global leader in digital entertainment.

3. Amazon and Expansion into New Markets: Amazon started as an online bookstore but has expanded into a variety of industries, including e-commerce, cloud services, and streaming. The company's ability to adapt and diversify has allowed it to grow and lead several markets.

4. Tesla and Overcoming Production Challenges: Tesla faced several production challenges during its early years, but the company adapted and found solutions to overcome these obstacles. Constant innovation and perseverance have helped Tesla establish itself as a leader in the electric vehicle industry.

Overcoming Challenges and Changes

Challenges and changes are inevitable on the entrepreneurial journey. Here are some tips for overcoming these challenges and adapting successfully:

1. Maintain a Long-Term Perspective: When facing challenges, maintain a long-term perspective. Remember that current obstacles are temporary and that your end goal is what matters. Having a clear vision of the future can help maintain motivation and resilience.

2. Learn from Failures and Mistakes: Instead of seeing failures as defeats, see them as learning opportunities. Analyze what went wrong, identify lessons learned, and apply that knowledge to improve in the future. The ability to learn from mistakes is an important part of resilience.

3. Seek Support and Guidance: Don't hesitate to seek support and guidance when needed. Talk to mentors, colleagues, and friends to get advice and different perspectives. Collaboration and support can help face challenges more effectively.

4. Maintain Emotional Balance: Managing your emotions is essential to dealing with changes and challenges. Practice emotional self-control techniques and maintain a positive attitude. The ability to remain calm and emotionally balanced can improve your ability to face adversity.

5. Adopt a Growth Mindset: Cultivate a growth mindset that sees challenges as opportunities to grow and develop new skills. Instead of focusing on failure, see each challenge as a chance to improve and evolve.

The Art of Being Resilient and Adaptable

Resilience and adaptation are essential skills for entrepreneurs looking to achieve long-term success. By facing challenges and changes with a positive and flexible mindset, you can overcome obstacles and seize opportunities that arise along the way. Developing resilience involves accepting reality, staying focused on goals and learning from experiences.

In this chapter, we explore the concept of resilience, strategies for developing this skill, and examples of how adaptation can lead to success. By adopting a resilient and adaptive approach, you will be better prepared to face challenges and create a path to lasting success.

The entrepreneurial journey is full of ups and downs, but with resilience and an adaptable mindset, you can turn challenges into opportunities and continue to grow and prosper. Hold firm to your goals, learn from your experiences, and continue moving toward success.

CHAPTER 15: LEGACY AND IMPACT: BUILDING A LASTING FUTURE

Reaching the end of the entrepreneurial journey is not just about achieving goals and objectives, but also about leaving a lasting legacy and having a significant impact on the world. In this chapter, we'll explore how to build a legacy that transcends your career and makes a positive difference in people's lives and in your industry. We'll look at how to create a lasting impact, strategies for leaving a meaningful legacy, and examples of leaders and entrepreneurs who have managed to do so.

The Meaning of Legacy

The concept of legacy goes beyond simple achievements and financial success. It's about leaving a brand that reflects your values, your contributions and your impact on people's lives. A lasting legacy is built not only through personal achievements, but also through the positive impact you have on society and the lives of those around you. Here are some essential aspects of a legacy:

1. **Values and Principles:** The legacy you leave behind is often a reflection of the values and principles you espoused throughout your life. These values shape your decisions and actions and influence how you are remembered. Maintaining integrity, ethics and responsibility in your actions is essential to building a positive legacy.

2. **Impact on the Community:** Building a legacy also involves contributing to the community and making a difference in people's lives. Supporting social causes, investing in community projects and promoting positive changes are ways to create a lasting impact.

3. **Inspiration for Others:** Your legacy can serve as a source of inspiration for others. Whether through your achievements, your stories of overcoming or your leadership principles, your example can motivate and influence future generations to follow in your footsteps and pursue their own goals.

4. **Contributions to the Sector:** In addition to impacting the community, your legacy can manifest itself through significant contributions to your sector or area of activity. Innovations, ethical business practices and positive industry changes are ways to leave a lasting mark.

Strategies for Building a Lasting Legacy

Building a lasting legacy requires a conscious and strategic approach. Here are some strategies to help create a meaningful impact and leave a legacy that resonates over time:

1. **Define Your Purpose and Vision:** Clarify the purpose and vision that guide your entrepreneurial journey. Ask yourself: "What is my mission?" and "How do I want to be remembered?" Having a clear vision and well-defined purpose will help direct your actions and ensure they are aligned with your long-term goals.

2. Prioritize Social Responsibility: Get involved in social responsibility initiatives and support causes that align with your values. Whether through donations, volunteering or partnerships with non-profit organizations, contribute to the improvement of society and the environment.

3. Invest in the Development of Others: Dedicate time and resources to mentor and develop other professionals. Share your knowledge, offer guidance, and create opportunities for others to grow and prosper. Investing in the success of others not only helps strengthen your community, it also contributes to a lasting legacy.

4. Promote Innovation and Continuous Improvement: Constantly seek innovations and improvements in your field of activity. Contribute new ideas and solutions that can transform your sector and benefit society. Continuous innovation and the pursuit of excellence are ways to leave a significant mark.

5. Document and Share Your Knowledge: Create a record of your knowledge and experience to share with future generations. Write books, give talks and participate in interviews to disseminate your ideas and contributions. Documenting and sharing your knowledge helps ensure your legacy continues to influence and inspire.

6. Create a Foundation or Social Project: Consider creating a foundation or social project that reflects your passions and values. This can be an effective way to make a lasting impact and continue contributing to important causes after your career.

7. Build a Legacy Culture in Your Organization: If you lead a company, encourage a culture that values and seeks to build a positive legacy. Establish practices and values that promote social responsibility, ethics and innovation within the organization.

Examples of Lasting Legacies

1. **Nelson Mandela and the Fight for Equality:** Nelson Mandela is an example of someone who left a lasting legacy through his fight for equality and justice. His commitment to peace and reconciliation in South Africa has had a global impact and continues to inspire people around the world to fight for human rights and social justice.

2. **Bill Gates and the Bill and Melinda Gates Foundation:** Bill Gates, co-founder of Microsoft, left a significant legacy through his philanthropic foundation. The Bill and Melinda Gates Foundation works to fight disease, improve education and reduce global poverty. The impact of your contributions continues to make a difference in many areas.

3. **Oprah Winfrey and Personal Empowerment:** Oprah Winfrey is known for her impact on personal empowerment and promoting well-being. Her career as a television host, author and philanthropist has inspired millions of people to pursue their dreams and make positive changes in their lives.

4. **Steve Jobs and the Technological Revolution:** Steve Jobs, co-founder of Apple, left a lasting legacy by transforming the technology industry with innovations like the iPhone and iPad. His vision and creativity have helped shape the way we interact with technology and have had a profound impact on many areas of everyday life.

Creating a Legacy that Stands the Test of Time

Building a lasting legacy requires a commitment to excellence and a focus on the contributions you can make to society and your industry. Here are some additional tips to ensure your legacy stands the test of time:

1. **Be Consistent and Authentic:** Maintain consistency in your actions and be authentic in your intentions. A lasting legacy is built on a solid foundation of integrity and authenticity. Stay true

to your values and principles throughout your journey.

2. Adapt and Evolve: The world is constantly changing, and a lasting legacy is one that adapts and evolves over time. Be open to new ideas and innovations, and look for ways to adjust your approach to continue making a positive impact.

3. Engage with the Community: Build strong relationships and collaborate with the community to understand their needs and contribute in a meaningful way. Building a support network and actively participating in the community helps strengthen your legacy and ensure it has a lasting impact.

4. Inspire the Next Generation: Share your vision and experience with the next generation of leaders and entrepreneurs. Inspire and motivate young people to pursue their own goals and contribute to society. The legacy you leave behind can be amplified through the actions and accomplishments of those you helped empower.

5. Reflect and Evaluate Regularly: Regularly reflect on the impact you are making and how you are progressing toward your legacy. Assess your accomplishments and identify areas where you can make improvements or adjustments. Maintaining a critical and open outlook will help ensure your legacy continues to evolve and make a difference.

Conclusion: The Lasting Impact of the Entrepreneurial Journey

Building a lasting legacy is the culmination of a successful and meaningful entrepreneurial journey. By focusing on your values, contributing to the community, driving innovation, and sharing your knowledge, you can create an impact that transcends your career and continues to positively influence the world.

In this chapter, we explore the meaning of legacy, strategies for building it, and examples of leaders who have made a lasting impact. Building a legacy involves a combination of commitment, adaptability and inspiration. By adopting these practices and continuing to look for ways to make a difference, you will be paving the way for a lasting and meaningful future.

Remember that true success is not just measured by individual achievements, but by the impact you have on people's lives and society as a whole. By building a positive legacy, you leave a mark that will continue to inspire and influence future generations.

THE PATH TO THE MILLIONAIRE MINDSET

As we close our journey through the principles and practices of the millionaire mindset, it is crucial to reflect on the path we have taken and the insights we have gained. What has become clear is that the millionaire mentality is not exclusive to a privileged few, but rather a philosophy accessible to everyone who is willing to embrace a new way of thinking and acting. Through the pages of this book, we explore how to cultivate a success mindset, overcome obstacles, and create lasting impact. Now, it's time to consolidate these teachings and understand how they can be applied in your own life.

Thinking Big: The First Step to Success

The millionaire mindset starts with the ability to think big. We encourage you to expand your horizons and imagine possibilities beyond the limitations we often impose on ourselves. Visionary thinking is the starting point for any significant endeavor. As we've discussed throughout the book, big achievements start with big dreams. Don't be afraid to dream big and visualize the success you want to achieve.

Develop expansive thinking It involves challenging your comfort zone and exploring new opportunities. Cultivating this mindset is an ongoing practice, and it is essential to be open to new ideas and possibilities. Great visionaries like Elon Musk and Richard Branson started with bold dreams that challenged the status quo. They showed that thinking big is the foundation for creating innovations and transforming industries. Your example reminds us that by allowing yourself to dream big, you open doors to extraordinary achievements.

Acting with Determination: Turning Visions into Reality

Thinking big is just the first step; Determination and action are the fuel that turns visions into reality. This book explored the importance of having a clear action plan and staying focused on goals. Determination is what drives you to move forward, even when you face obstacles and challenges.

Implement effective strategies and maintain persistence are fundamental to transforming your dreams into tangible achievements. The trajectory of successful entrepreneurs, such as Jeff Bezos and Oprah Winfrey, illustrates the importance of acting with determination and resilience. They faced adversity and persisted in their goals, which allowed them to achieve success. Your journey demonstrates that by staying focused and determined, you can overcome challenges and achieve your goals.

Never Give Up: The Key to Lasting Success

Resilience and the ability to never give up are central elements to the millionaire mindset. Throughout this book, we discuss how facing failure and adversity is an inevitable part of the entrepreneurial journey. Success is not a fixed destination, but a continuous process of learning and growth.

View failures as learning opportunities and staying committed to your goals are practices that strengthen your ability to persevere. Examples such as Thomas Edison, who persisted after countless failed attempts to invent the electric light bulb, show that persistence is essential for success. His dedication and resilience not only led to the invention of one of the greatest technological milestones, but also illustrates the importance of never giving up.

The Lasting Impact of the Millionaire Mindset

Finally, the millionaire mindset is not just about financial success, but also about the positive impact you can have on your life and the lives of those around you. Building a lasting legacy involves applying the principles of the millionaire mindset to make a difference in the world. It's about being a leader who inspires and contributes to the well-being of the community and society.

Leave a positive legacy it is the result of a mindset that not only seeks personal success, but also seeks to contribute to the greater good. Leaders such as Nelson Mandela and Bill Gates show that true impact goes beyond personal achievements and is reflected in the contribution to society and the strengthening of communities.

In Summary: The Journey of the Millionaire Mindset

As you reflect on the key points covered in this book, remember that the millionaire mindset is accessible to anyone who is willing to commit to a broad vision, act with determination, and never give up. Developing this mindset is an ongoing journey of personal and professional growth, and the practices and strategies discussed here are valuable tools to help you achieve success.

Get inspired by the stories and examples presented and apply the principles of the millionaire mindset to your own life. Remember that every challenge is an opportunity to grow and every obstacle is a chance to become stronger. By embracing big thinking, determination, and resilience, you'll be on your way to achieving your goals and leaving a lasting legacy.

The millionaire mindset is more than a set of practices; is a life philosophy that empowers you to turn dreams into reality and create meaningful impact. Continue to think big, act with determination and never give up. The path to success is an ongoing journey, and the millionaire mindset is the key to unlocking your maximum potential.

www.ingramcontent.com/pod-product-compliance
Lightning Source LLC
Chambersburg PA
CBHW050323230526
45471CB00005B/2315